MW00618603

POWER of
PRACTICE

*How to Transform Your Life
by Practicing Every Day*

Copyright © 2017 by Saydeah E. Howard

All rights reserved. No part of this book may be reproduced or transmitted in any form or by any means without written permission from the author.

ISBN 978-1-944623-02-9

Book design by Kim Dow, dowhouse.com

This book is dedicated to *you*.
To the present you and the future *you*.
The *you* you want to be.
The *you* you know you can be.
The *you* you are destined to be.
This is your *opportunity* to make choices
that serve your future self.
The *self* you want to be.
The *self* you know you can be.
You deserve this because you're worth it.
I wrote this for *you*.

Contents

Introduction

I WAS TALKING WITH A FRIEND RECENTLY ABOUT NEW YEAR'S RESOLUTIONS AND WHY I DON'T MAKE THEM. WE WERE DISCUSSING THE NUMBER OF BOOKS I READ LAST year, and she was saying how impressed she was that I had actually stuck with my New Year's resolution to read more. I tried to explain that I don't make New Year's resolutions, that I don't believe they actually work when it comes to changing behavior. My friend insisted that's what I'd done, though, pointing out that I'd *resolved* to do something, and I'd accomplished that goal in time for the start of the New Year. Hence, a New Year's resolution.

Touché. She had a point.

I sat with the conversation for a long time afterward, wondering why I had such a visceral negative reaction to the idea of this type of resolution. Was it because studies tell us over and over that we're all doomed to fail when we set resolutions at the beginning of each year? Was it because I had experienced so much failure in the past and didn't want to be associated with that failure? Was it because I studied organizational change in graduate school and understood how hard it is to create real and lasting change? And if all of that was true, why the heck would I write yet another book about keeping New Year's resolutions?

We all know New Year's resolutions are bullshit. Sorry for the profanity, but let's call it what it is. Every year we say we're going to do these things, but we don't. Or we do them for a while and stop. If we really want to do them, why wait until the first of the year? If you know you want to lose weight and it's November, then why not *start in November*, right?

Just because Thanksgiving is coming up doesn't mean you can't start practicing good habits then. In fact, that's actually the perfect time to put into action the changes you want to make, especially if they are really going to be long-term changes and not just short-term bursts of activity. There's no benefit to saying you're *waiting* for January 1st, other than continuing to lie to yourself.

But if I truly feel that way, why do I do it? Why have I started something new at the beginning of each year for the past seven years, and why do I continue to do it?

Ultimately, I think asking why I do it is less important

than asking why and how I've been so successful at it. How have I managed to achieve the goals I've set for myself at the start of each year for seven years running?

ADD, NOT SUBTRACT

One of the reasons I've been successful in accomplishing my yearly goals is that my approach is different from the way people usually think about resolutions. Resolutions are often centered around eliminating things from one's life—subtraction. They're about losing weight, or cutting out sweets, or no longer drinking. Although I didn't realize it when I started, I've never made a goal whose focus was to get me to *stop* doing something. Subtraction was never my intent. From the first day of the first year, it has always been about *adding* something to my life.

My goals are about making myself better in some small way by taking on new habits or new activities that may make me happier, but more importantly, that I feel will enhance my life. Each year as I start to think about what comes next, my approach is, *What do I want to give myself this year?* and not, *What do I want to take away?* I think of what I want to add to my life, not how I want to punish myself. (And that is what New Year's Resolutions often feel like to me: punishment).

I always think it's strange when people try to find ways to deprive themselves or punish themselves. Wouldn't you rather look for gifts to give yourself for the next year and beyond? Wouldn't you rather find a way to enhance your life?

TIMELESS

Okay, so you've decided you want to add something to your life—great, but why do it at the start of the year? One of the reasons I start on January 1 is because I like the simple structure of a calendar year. My brain resonates with a structured period of time and a year makes it easy to do that. It's a long enough stretch to know if something really is going to stick as a habit for the rest of my life or not, but it is not so long that it feels impossible or interminable. It's also another way to reflect on growing older and hopefully getting better as each year passes. Had I really thought about it more seven years ago I would have started on my birthday, since that would be a natural demarcation of growth and development from year to year.

On a practical level, I track what I do, so having an annual calendar also makes it easier to do that. As I will discuss later, however, you don't have to set your daily practice for a year, or even a month, for real change to happen. The key isn't 365 days or when in the year you start. The magic is in practicing daily. So I recommend choosing whatever time frame works best for you and sticking with it. Don't get stuck on the time; what's important is committing to doing whatever you've chosen to do every day. If you're scared and unsure you can make it through a whole month or year, start with seven days. Plan on doing something every day for seven days in a row and build from there.

And that is precisely why I wrote this book—because I want to help you find the methods and tools that will help you to be successful. I recognize that my journey will not be the same as yours, but I believe the lessons I've learned will help you as you embark on your own road to change. Not everything I've been through will resonate with you, however, so when I tell you what I've done you will have to stop and think about how that applies to you and what will work in your life. This is the time to stop talking about change and start doing something about it, and my hope is that this guide will be a great starting point to get you going.

This book is for the people who keep talking about change but can't seem to make it happen. It's for people that see the possibility of a different life for themselves but can't get over the hump of fear and doubt and all the excuses that hold us back from success. That was me for a very long time. I was unable to finish anything I started. I dreamed of a different world, a different me, but didn't know how to get there. And sometimes—and I think this is even worse—I knew *how* to make it happen, but couldn't find the motivation to *make* it happen.

If you are like I was, this book is for you. I want to share my experiences with trying and failing, as well as my experiences with trying and succeeding. I've finally figured out how to succeed in doing the things I want to be doing, and I would like to help you do that as well. I've changed my life—and if I can do it, I know you can too.

THE SECRET

So, what is the magic sauce? What finally changed to make these things possible? The good and bad news is that nothing changed and everything changed.

"Nothing changed" in that there wasn't a magic bullet, big secret, or divine revelation that made everything better. Spoiler alert: There is no magic involved in change. There is no big epiphany that I dazzle you with at the end of this book that changes your life. True change begins with just a few simple tweaks and guidelines that anyone and everyone can embrace. It starts with being intentional about the change we want, practicing that change, and finding ways to incorporate it in our lives every day.

When I said that everything changed, what I mean is, I finally *wanted* it. I finally wanted change to happen. Actually, really wanted it. I wanted it more than I wanted to complain about it. I wanted it more than I dreaded whatever temporary pain I would have to experience in order to get there. I wanted it more than I wanted to sleep in, or watch a bad TV show, or eat something that wasn't good for me. I wanted it enough that I was willing to spend my time in a different way and intentionally make different choices.

If you are there, and if you want change more than you want those other things, it's time for you to read this book. This book won't give you the *want*, but if you already have the desire, I can give you some tips, ideas, and suggestions for how to make that change happen. I hope you find the success you're looking for and the success you deserve. I congratulate you on taking the first step in the process. I wish you the best of luck in your transformation—and if you adopt a daily intentional practice, I'm certain you'll make it happen. Good luck, and let's get started!

1.

Resolution to Intention

DOES THE WORLD NEED YET ANOTHER BOOK THAT TELLS US HOW TO CHANGE, HOW TO BE HAPPY, AND HOW TO LIVE? PROBABLY NOT. AND WHAT MAKES SOMEONE ELSE qualified to tell others how to do those things? I'm not sure about you, but I don't know anyone who's happy all the time, or who's figured out how to never make mistakes and is living their best life, being their best self, every single minute of every single day. Maybe Tony Robbins has it all figured out—I've never seen that guy down—but for the rest of us, who really has it together all the time? Certainly not me.

So, what makes me qualified to write a book on making real changes and living the best life possible? As Marianne Williamson writes in her book *A Return to Love*, "Our deepest fear is not that we are inadequate. Our deepest fear is that we are powerful beyond measure." Think about that for a moment. You are powerful beyond measure. Even in those moments when you're scared and unsure, you are powerful.

I struggle with this one often. I'm scared. All the time. Of so many things. I was scared to write this book. I'm still scared to share it with the world. Scared of the criticism I will receive. Scared of letting people in. Scared of losing my privacy and anonymity. Like I said, I'm scared of a lot of things. But Williamson is right: my fear isn't that I am inadequate, it is that I am actually more powerful than I think.

In this passage, Williamson goes on to say, "We ask ourselves, who am I to be brilliant, gorgeous, talented, fabulous? Actually, who are you not to be? You are a child of God. Your playing small does not serve the world." When I read that line—"your playing small does not serve the world"—I had to stop and ask myself if that was true. I quickly realized that it was. Not only are we all more powerful than we think, shying away from our talent does not serve us or the world.

Lastly, Williamson says, "We are all meant to shine, as children do. We were born to make manifest the glory of God that is within us. It is not just in some of us; it's in everyone. And as we let our own light shine, we unconsciously give others permission to do the same. As we are liberated from our own fear, our presence automatically liberates others." So, I'm letting my light shine. I'm showing my glory to the world in the hope that it helps someone else find theirs. I'm not an expert, I'm no sage, but I am someone who has been doing this successfully for seven years, with no plans to stop. This isn't a one-time, hokey thing for publicity or fame. This is a real part of my life that has helped me greatly, and if stepping out into the world and sharing my story helps others, who am I to fear that? Who am I to hide my light?

EMBRACING CHANGE

So, you want to change yourself? You want to grow and transform? It should be simple: 1) Buy this book 2) Read this book 3) Do what this book says.

Well, if it really was that easy we would all be enlightened, emotionally healthy, skinny millionaires. The reality is that change is hard. Period. And it's often scary and hard to start—especially for people who don't know where to begin. And sometimes even when you do know where to start, navigating your way through change and knowing what to do when your plans go out the window can be even harder.

Allow me a moment to digress. Because of my unusual name, people often ask me where I'm from, and it's never an easy answer. I usually say something like "all over" or "I've lived everywhere." The truth is, I grew up with constant change because my family moved all the time. I was born in Monrovia, Liberia and emigrated to the United States when I was young. We initially lived in Washington, DC, then in Maryland, and then Virginia. Later we moved to Oklahoma City; then Enid, Oklahoma; and then Fort Worth, Texas, which is where I finished high school. We moved every year when I was growing up, and I don't remember going to the same school twice until my sophomore and junior years of high school.

As an extremely shy and introverted child, I found this constant change both terrifying and effortless. The terrifying part was having to get used to a new school, new teachers, and new kids every single year. The effortless part was, I wasn't leaving friends in the old place and knew I probably wouldn't make friends in the new one, so there was no deep sense of loss when we moved. Nothing was really going to be different in my world, regardless of where we were moving to, so our relocations didn't bother me much.

Change was such a constant for me that it became my routine. When I got to a new town, I knew it was likely that I would be gone the next year, so I didn't really work at modifying things. Rather, I focused on simply getting used to the new routine for the year and getting on with my life.

To my surprise, what I found was that every year I came out of my shell a bit more. I was a little less shy with each move. And then the strangest thing started to happen: every time we moved it got a little tougher, because I had actually made friends. I had gotten to know people and I was growing. Change was slow, but it was definitely happening. And it was happening because, without realizing it, I had embraced change over the years.

THE WEIGHT

One of the most common areas of change people often focus on is related to losing weight. I know this battle personally, having been anywhere from overweight to obese at different points in my life.

While I wasn't a skinny kid, I was never really big, or even what you would call chubby. After puberty I started putting on weight, but that was nothing compared to what happened after I graduated from college and began working at a very stressful job. I worked a lot of hours during those years, and spent most of them sitting hunched over a computer screen. Add to that a pretty unhealthy diet, and it's no surprise how quickly I gained weight. By a couple of years into my early twenties, I was between fifty and sixty pounds overweight.

Things only got worse when I moved to Los Angeles and entered the entertainment industry, where destructive body images were a constant. After a short time in LA, I promised myself that I would lose the weight, and started making a concerted effort to do so.

The good news is, I've lost a significant amount of weight twice in my life. The bad news is, I had to lose it *twice*, because I gained it all back the first time.

The first time I lost a significant amount of weight, I stopped eating and started working out all the time. No joke, over a three-month period I barely ate one meal a day and often worked out twice a day.

I don't recommend that approach for a variety of reasons—the primary one being that it's the easiest and quickest way to gain the weight right back, plus some extra. Trust me, I know from personal experience. In fact, by the time I relocated from Los Angeles back to the Bay Area, I weighed well over 200 pounds. For those who know me now, or if you've looked at my author photo, this is probably a surprise. For reference, I'm five feet six inches, which means that at over 200 pounds, I was officially overweight and bordering on obese. I stopped weighing myself when I realized the number was over 200, so I'm not really sure how big I got at my heaviest.

The second time I lost the weight I did it the right way: slowly, over time, and with a balance of eating better and moderate exercise. Doing it the right way was hard, but absolutely worth it for my health and self-esteem. I've found that the things you often want the most are usually hard and require some amount of work. If you're not ready for that, then you may not be ready for change yet—and that's okay. We all start when we're truly ready. One of the most important elements to creating change is the true and real desire to change. There are many paths to creating change and they all start at the same place: *wanting* change to happen.

YOUR JOURNEY IS A GIFT

My story is about spending 365 days of the year (or 366, in leap years) making transformation happen. Your story doesn't have to be that, however; your story can be whatever works for you. The key is to make it intentional, do it daily, and focus on the practices that work best for you. This is a phrase you'll hear me use often in this book, because, as a former boss of mine was fond of saying, "We're all unique snowflakes, with no one else exactly like us." That means there is no one-size-fits-all solution for making change happen. It's about figuring out what is right for you. So if starting out with a 365-day timeline seems like too much, don't do it. Start with whatever timeframe works for you and grow it from there. You can try for forty days of joy, where you do one joyful thing each day, or ninety days of gratitude, or two weeks of eating healthy—whatever works for you, that's your starting point. The goal is to stop talking about what you want to do and start doing it.

As the sun comes up each morning, we are given another opportunity to see a new day. How do you think about the day? Is each new sunrise a gift to you, or a burden? It only came to me recently, as I was struggling through heartbreak and unhappiness with my job, that each day I wake up and am able to take a breath is a gift—and it's one that I squander most days. Why is that? Why do we often take for granted that we will see more sunrises and sunsets and not appreciate the precious moments in between? Well, I am trying to do just that these days—really focus on how to make the most of each moment I have, from the time I wake up to the time I go to sleep. I'm not perfect—in fact, I'm far from it—but in asking myself to be aware of that fact, and making an effort to change just a few things in my life, I am better able to live in the moment and appreciate what I have.

What are you going to do with the gift you've been given today?

Maybe you're not ready for what you've been dreaming about to actually come true. That's okay. If you've sat down and had a real moment of introspection and you're really not ready to do the hard work, don't beat yourself up. Change is a process that is often not a straight road. You may start and stop and experience failure along the way. But those aren't really failures; they are opportunities to figure out what works for you and what doesn't. And that is where this book can make an impact: it can help get you started on the road to understanding different approaches to change, through the lens of my own trial and error. My message is simple: Don't quit. No matter the setbacks and failures, look at them as learning opportunities, experiments that have taught you something, and find ways to keep going.

BE INTENTIONAL

So, how do you get started? The first step is being aware of what you're doing right now. In order to be intentional about making different choices, we have to know what choices we're currently making. How often are you aware of what you're doing, in the moment you're doing it? More important, are you thinking about *why* you're doing it? If not, why not? When you're eating something that's not good for you are you doing it mindlessly, stuffing handful after handful in your mouth? That is not being present. That is not intentionality.

Before you can tackle the changes you want to make, you have to understand what you're currently doing. A friend shared Sarah Knight's TED Talk, *"The Life Changing Magic of Not Giving a F*ck,"* with me, and I was blown away—not just by her ability to drop F-bombs at will, but also by the simple brilliance of her message. Your "fucks," Knight says, are the time, energy, and money you spend on things in life. She advises you to stop spending your time, energy, and money on things you don't want to spend it on. If you don't want to go to a friend's baby shower, for example, it's okay to say no. I love Sarah's message because it starts with the idea of being aware of what you're doing, with your energy, your money, and especially your time.

When we know what we're doing, we can examine what we want to change. For you, is it how you spend your time, money, or energy? Whatever area you want to focus on, once you've actually taken time to study these things and understand what you're currently doing, you can identify what you want to change and create a plan for how to do that.

Start by digging into what's going on for you right now. It's a tall order to look at *every*thing in your life, so start with some of the most important things, like how you're spending your time, energy, and money. Get aware with yourself on these things, and you'll be on the path to creating intention in what you're doing.

PRACTICE, PRACTICE, PRACTICE

Once you've cultivated an awareness of what you're doing, you'll need to start doing something different, which brings in the second element of my approach: practice. Yes, Allen Iverson, "we're talking about practice." If you remember his 2002 rant responding to criticism of his lack of effort in practice before games, you're probably laughing right now, but this is a critical issue. "Practice makes perfect" is a saying for a reason. Stephen Curry, who's won multiple league MVPs and NBA Championships, practices his ball handling skills in the same way before every single game, because he recognizes that his success is based on a steadfast focus on the fundamentals of building good habits. The same applies to world-class chefs like Bobby Flay or Alex Guarnaschelli, both Food Network stars, they practice their cooking skills on a regular basis in order to stay at the top of their craft. Even when you're at the top of your game, daily practice is necessary. It may not be exciting, but fundamentals, made strong over time through practice, win championships.

DO IT DAILY

Lastly, you need to combine the awareness of what you're doing with the actions you want to take, and *practice them on a daily basis.* Why daily and not every once in a while, or when you can fit it in? Because while "occasionally" may help in changing some things, I can guarantee it won't work as well as committing yourself to a daily practice. Think of the things you do every once in a while versus those you do every day. Which are you better at? Especially when you're first learning something new, the consistency of pushing yourself to engage in it with every circle of the sun is invaluable. Even something as simple as using your password at work. You don't even think about it as you enter it every day, but if you go away on vacation and actually check out for a while, you may, as I do, forget your password when you first come back to the office. Intentional, daily practice cements actions into your routine in a way that nothing else will.

Each day contains a finite number of hours, minutes, and seconds. Are you aware of what you're doing with those precious seconds? Are you leaving the TV on, or are you going for the walk you promised yourself you would? Are you grabbing the croissant or taking the apple? Are you conscious of what you're doing and making different choices? You can stay on Facebook for ten more minutes, or you can get offline and read that book or call a friend. Are you being intentional in those moments? What would happen if you were? What would happen if you chose just one thing to be intentional about and did that thing every day of your life for a fixed period of time? Think of the ways in which your life could change, grow, and get better if you did.

2.
Habits

AMONG MANY DEFINITIONS, ACCORDING TO WEBSTER'S DICTIONARY, A HABIT IS "A BEHAVIOR PATTERN ACQUIRED THROUGH FREQUENT OR PHYSIOLOGIC EXPOSURE THAT shows itself in regularity or increased facility of performance" or an "acquired mode of behavior that has become nearly or completely involuntary."

What does that actually mean? Essentially, habits are repeated behaviors that have become automatic.

If habits are ingrained or automatic behaviors, how do you change or eliminate bad ones—and, more important, how do you build good ones? Let's start by looking at a few habits we all have. For example, how much are you really thinking when you brush your teeth? Do you think about how you put the toothpaste on your toothbrush when you brush your teeth in the morning, or does that somehow happen unconsciously? When you take a shower, you probably have a certain washing order you go through, but are you stopping to think about it every time you step under the water? What about which shoe you put on first when you're getting ready? Or which pant leg you step through first?

These are all habits—actions that are so automatic that our active brains turn off as we perform them. And we all have more habits than we realize, because we've done them over and over again. Hopefully, we're brushing our teeth, taking a shower, and getting dressed every day, so we no longer think about these tasks anymore. We no longer need to practice any of these activities, because they're ingrained. Just like muscle memory that develops with specific sports, like running or lifting weights, your body and mind know what to do when you're engaged in those activities.

What if you could use that same idea to change other areas of your life? What if you did something every single day; could it make a difference in your life?

CUE, ROUTINE, REWARD

Charles Duhigg's book *The Power of Habits* is a fascinating read that explores both the scientific research around habit formation and how to change habits. I recommend checking it out to get deeper insight into the topic. A woefully brief summary of his work is that habits work on a cue, routine, and reward loop, and if you can determine what your cue is and change the routine to get to the reward, you can create a new habit or change an existing one. When thinking about my daily intentional practice journey, I realized that a lot of Duhigg's theories are relevant to what I've done over the past seven years, all long before reading his fascinating book. Without realizing it, I've utilized most of the tools he advocates for to effect habit formation or change.

The second part of the definition of a habit speaks to the point that they are actions that have become involuntary at some point—and as with most things, some of the habits we have are good, while others are bad.

Let's go back to the toothpaste example, or how you tie your shoes. Those movements are likely automatic for you at this point in your life. You're not stopping to think about each step in the process, each movement your hand is making. But there was likely a time (probably when you were young) when you did have to think about how you brushed your teeth. Someone probably showed you how to slowly put the toothpaste on the toothbrush without it falling off; that same someone likely warned you not to swallow as you were brushing and to spit as you went along. It probably took you a few times of going through the process to stop thinking about how you were doing it, but now the entire thing is simply natural for you. You don't think about whether you'll start on the right side or the left, or in the middle of your mouth—you just start. No one needs to remind you to spit as you go or not to swallow toothpaste.

So many other elements of your day are daily habits that you probably don't even think about them anymore. When you drive to a new job for the first time, you're aware of every turn down each new street. When you've been driving there for four or five years, however, you stop noticing these things; in fact, I bet you sometimes get to work without even realizing it, because you've been on auto-pilot the whole time. That's what habits do: they eliminate the need for active thinking and let you relax, to some extent, because what you're doing is so automatic.

BUILDING NEW HABITS

When you try to do something new you use new skills, active thinking, and, technically speaking, the prefrontal cortex of your brain. You must exhibit a significant amount of thought and with it, control, to successfully accomplish a new task.

The same applies if you're trying to break a habit. You end up spending the majority of your effort on preventing yourself from doing something—and if you're spending a lot of energy and time working on *not* doing something you're exerting a lot of self-control and discipline, which takes a tremendous amount of energy out of you.

Wouldn't it be great to use your energy on something you really *want* to do versus focusing on something you *don't* want to do? If you're going to use the part of your brain that drains you the most, why not use it to create a new habit that actually adds to your life rather than trying to *stop* yourself from doing something?

This is where focused practice comes in. A daily intentional practice can help you create a new habit and is one of the building blocks you can use to achieve bigger goals. When we focus on creating a habit, versus trying to exert tremendous amounts of self-control and discipline to stop doing something, we are often more successful. According to Duhigg, replacing the routine in the habit loop can create not just change but real, lasting change.

Hopefully, it's clear by now how a daily intentional practice is different from a New Year's resolution. When you make a resolution, you're taking an action to fix a problem or making an effort to address a problem—and that's not what we're doing here. Take, for example, one of the most common resolutions we all focus on: losing weight. Actually, the *goal* is to lose weight; the *resolution* is to go on a diet or go to the gym, or other tangible actions that will help us to lose the weight. We focus on fixing something we perceive as wrong or focus on taking away something in order to fix something. But that starts with the premise that something is wrong with us to begin with—that something is broken within us and needs to be fixed. What would happen if the focus wasn't on what's wrong but on what we want to *add* to the equation? Why do we often think focusing on the negative gets us to improvement, instead of focusing on improvement by addition to begin with?

GIFTS AND SMALL WINS

In my job, I frequently conduct candidate references, and one of my standard questions is, "What have you identified as areas of improvement for the candidate?" I frame the question this way because I've found that references are often more willing to talk about development areas when the conversation is oriented around the idea of improvement versus what's "wrong" with the person, or what their "weaknesses" are. No matter how great the candidate, if they truly are a rock star they always want to be better, and knowing what areas of improvement they've already identified for themselves is the best way to set them up for success in the future.

As I make a commitment to myself at the start of each year, I tend to think about these intentions as a gift to myself, as a way to continue my improvement and development—because to be able to recognize the areas of yourself and of your life that you can grow, and then to be able to do something about it, truly *is* a gift. I don't think of myself as the world's best gift giver, but I do enjoy giving and receiving thoughtful gifts from close friends. And that is why I think of this practice as a daily gift to myself. Every day I get the opportunity to give myself the gift of time, the gift of activities that I enjoy, that feed my soul, and that truly make me happy. What better gift is there than that?

I also think of my daily intentional practice as a gift to myself because there's no sense of all or nothing in order to be successful. This is in contrast to resolutions, which sometimes carry a notion of, "I must do it all or I've failed." If we're focused on taking something away, for example—like sweets—the moment we have one bite of a piece of candy or cake, we've failed with our resolution. And once we tell ourselves we've failed, it's easier to give up entirely. So we go from "I'm not going to eat any sweets whatsoever" to "Oh no, I ate a bite of cake. Well, now that I've failed, I might as well eat an entire cake."

The all-or-nothing mentality isn't conducive to slow, gradual change, which we know is the best way to create a habit, which is what leads to lasting change. If you set yourself up for a big "all or nothing" moment and fail, you're not going to build your confidence and belief that you can actually achieve your goals. From Duhigg's *The Power of Habit,* we learn that we create permanent change by learning new routines and changing our habit loop, and we can do this by adding a new competing response—an alternative in the habit loop—that moves us in a different direction.

From Duhigg we also learn that "small wins through a steady application of small advantages fuel the transformative changes by leveraging tiny advantages into patterns that convince people that bigger achievements are within reach." Which is to say: Try not to set yourself up for all-or-nothing failures. Small wins give us a taste of success and help us begin to build a foundation that we can use later. Big wins in the form of completed goals are great, but they don't happen immediately. It's the small steps that, with each day of practice, turn into small wins, that gets us there. And we have to use the power of practice to get there.

When we focus on a daily intentional practice, we can recognize that every moment, within every day, is a chance to change things, to do something different. One of the most powerful mantras I've used in my life when trying to change my eating habits is the very simple notion of every meal being an opportunity to do the right thing. If you were to think of every time you sat down to eat as a chance to make the choices you want to make, how would that change your eating habits? What if you applied that same thinking to everything else you did in life?

Every morning you wake up is a new opportunity to start working out, just as your evenings at home after work are an opportunity to read, or study, or practice the guitar, or do anything else you want to do in life that you're not doing now. What will you do with that opportunity? What are you doing with those opportunities, with those precious moments? If you don't do it one day, rather than wasting time beating yourself up about it, simply forgive yourself and recognize that if you wake up again tomorrow, you will have another chance to do it.

Another reason I like the idea of daily intentions is that an intention is much more compassionate than a resolution. Intentions help us bring mindfulness to our actions—which I learned from a year of meditation, is so very important to our day-to-day happiness. Being aware of what you're doing and conscious of why you're doing it, is the key not only to happiness but to accomplishing the goals we set for ourselves. Like I said at the beginning of this book, this is hard, and it requires something different from what you've done before. Awareness is one of the keys to achieving the things you want.

Intentions ask us to do better rather than demanding we hold ourselves to unreasonable standards. Intentions are a promise we to make to our higher self, the self we want to be. Our future self. Intentions ask us to make different choices, and they allow us to engage in what we're trying to do. When we have an intention, we start from a place of belief and optimism. This is what we want to do; this is what we hope to do. This is our intention. Viewed this way, we can be less self-critical and give ourselves room to perform, not to mention leeway to start over, when necessary, without judgment. In those moments when we don't meet our intention we can begin again fresh, with that same optimism and openness rather than self-recrimination and pain.

Intentions and daily practices give us a chance to move on from moments where we didn't meet the opportunity presented us and look to the next moment. Because that next moment is another opportunity to do something different. Remember, tomorrow is a brand-new day, and you can always start again. What are you going to do with your next opportunity?

CHANGE INITIATIVES

In 2011 I obtained a Masters of Science in organizational development from the University of San Francisco (USF). I had always wanted to get a graduate degree, but I never knew what I wanted to study. I thought about business school and getting my MBA, but that never felt like the right fit. I was interested in studying leadership and teams, not poring over spreadsheets and profit-and-loss statements. It wasn't until I learned about organizational development that I realized there was a whole area of study that focused on how and why people work—and, more specifically, how organizations and teams work and how to get them to change when necessary.

Organizational development looks at how companies successfully and effectively create long-lasting change. Whether that is changing the culture or product or service offering, getting a group of people to collectively change the direction in which they're currently moving is a huge undertaking. It is made even more difficult when you think about how challenging it is to get one individual to make a change, much less a group of people with their own agendas, ideas, and biases.

One of the most important lessons I learned in my graduate program is that even when you have everyone on the same page and aligned with the need for change, you still have to get everyone to agree on what change is needed. What needs to be different, exactly? And how do we get there? Even when you know where you want to be, it's unlikely everyone will start out in agreement on which road they should take to get there. Add to that the challenge of everyone being in alignment on the methods behind the how, and you can see that creating change in an organization is a difficult task.

Finally, you have to address the people that want to derail the process. Some people will refuse to believe that change is necessary; others will not agree with the methods that have been identified to make it happen and will want to do it differently. Companies also sometimes have people who agree with the need for change but not what the ultimate goal is, so they will take over the process to get to their desired end result.

Given all of these challenges it is no wonder that change initiatives fail more often than they succeed. I find studying this dynamic fascinating, especially when you pull back from the study of the organization and just think about individuals and how we create change in our lives. I have always been interested in why some people are able to meet the goals they've outlined for themselves when it comes to growth and change and others are not. How can we expect organizations to change if we as individuals find it so hard to stop drinking, lose weight, start working out, or attain most of our objectives?

My goal with this book is to help others create behavioral change on an individual level, by providing the tools needed to do just that. As Socrates said, "The secret to change is to focus all your energy, not on fighting the old, but building the new." That is why I focus on things that will make me better, and not something I'm trying to stop.

What can you add to your toolbox that will help you achieve behavioral change? What do you want to add today?

EVERY TIME, EVERY DAY

As I mentioned, Duhigg talks about the habit loop consisting of three things: a cue, a routine, and reward. One of the most common examples of this loop in action is something that millions of people, probably including you, experience each morning—that first cup of coffee.

Think about your morning coffee for a minute.

That rush of caffeine that instantly puts you in a better mood and increases your energy. Now you're ready to tackle the day.

I'm not a coffee drinker, so my habit loop has a different look to it. It starts with a cue that I'm feeling a little sluggish, so I want sugar. My routine is to eat a donut or something with sugar, rather than caffeine. The reward is the rush of sugar and energy hitting my bloodstream, very similar to the boost that one gets with their morning coffee. The boost is part of the benefit, but the actual reward is the feeling of warmth, comfort, and familiarity I get with my sugar routine. It reminds me of happy moments in my childhood, times when I felt safe and loved.

The same often happens for others with their morning coffee ritual. It's not just the physical caffeine effect, it's all the other emotional elements of the routine. Those additional benefits are a hard reward to mimic in other ways, but figuring out what the cue is and changing the routine in a manner that will still allow me to get to that same warm and safe feeling is the only way I'll ever break my sugar cravings. That feeling has become so ingrained in my mind that it's almost automatic now for me: when I'm feeling stressed or tired, I reach for something sweet. It's become such a habit that "addiction" is the more accurate description at this point. If you're a coffee drinker, you may have thought of your morning (or afternoon) coffee as an addiction at some point as well.

So, now that we have a better understanding of how we can create new habits you may ask once again, why a *daily* goal? Why can't I just do this thing once or twice a week? Well, as theologian Mike Murdock says, "You will never change your life until you change something you do daily. The secret of your future is hidden in your daily routine." While I may not agree with much more of what Dr. Murdock preaches, I do 100 percent agree that the things you do each day tell a bigger story about your life and future than you realize. As entrepreneur and coach Zack Jones discussed in a recent Medium article about resolutions, the key is not to dream smaller or lower yourself to "realistic goals"; the key is to fundamentally change the way we do things, and that starts by practicing every day.

When you set out to do something only two or three days a week, it becomes too easy to miss that goal a few times—and now you're not accomplishing anything. This inevitably leads to you spending more time beating yourself up about it than trying to do better, or even to your giving up altogether. It is a way to prevent yourself from actually changing your life, because you're not making any real changes to your daily routine—and remember, your daily routine *is* your life. You're not actually doing the hard thing, which is to do something differently. It's too easy to say tomorrow, or the day after that when it's not consistent. Say today, and *every* day, if you want to make something a true part of your life. Make it a daily routine and it will become your life.

The things we do with each moment of our day—working out, going to work, reading a book, watching TV, walking the dog, spending time with friends or family members—that is our life, plain and simple. If you dream of changing some aspect of your life, you will need to start by changing what you do with each of those precious moments in the day—and you need to do it every day, not just two to three times a week. That's the only way to truly see results.

Think about how you might have made New Year's resolutions in the past, and how you didn't keep them. This year doesn't have to be like that. This year, you will have the tools necessary to commit to making real behavioral change happen. As Jones and I both say, "If we're serious about improving our lives, we need to make a daily habit." This approach changes the way we think about our goal and alters what a regular day looks like every day, not just those "special" days two or three times a week.

Supposedly, Einstein's definition of insanity was expecting different results from doing the same thing. Have you been doing the same thing for years, but hoping for different results? Change requires different thinking and different action. It demands designing a new way of doing things. If you want different results, you have to do something different today. And every day after that.

It is easier to commit to starting today if you tell yourself there is no tomorrow to put something off to. Every day we're able to draw new breath is a new opportunity. How will you reconfigure your life to incorporate whatever it is you want to do? In my case, I wanted to write every day this year, but between a very demanding job, my desire to exercise and read every day, and the fact that I'd actually like to see my friends every once in a while, I was really scared and confused about how I was going to find the time to do it. So I started the way I start with all of my daily intentional practice ideas—by asking myself if it was something I really wanted. Because you have to have the want, in a real and true way, if you're going to be able to do this.

My answer was yes, without hesitation, which told me I was willing to do something, or even a few things, differently in order to achieve that goal. The next step was to look at my daily patterns and see where I could realistically make time to write. I didn't establish a specific word count or time goal from the beginning; my only goal was to write every single day. So I looked at my calendar and thought about when in my day I could consistently and reliably set aside at least a few minutes to do that. I'm a morning person, so I knew that trying to do it at the end of the day was not going to work. I initially thought about waking up earlier and writing before the gym, but my alarm already goes off at 5:00 a.m., and there's not a whole lot earlier I could wake up and still be happy about it.

I also wanted to write when I had the most energy and mental focus to give to it, without worrying about work emails I wasn't responding to, or a lot of other distractions demanding my attention. With this in mind, I realized that my happiest and most productive moments in the day are often after my workout and shower and before I start my day—so, that's when I decided to write. It has meant going into the office a little later and staying there later, but it's worth it to know that I'll have this time, however long it is, to sit and do something that I love—something that gives me the reward I crave at the end of every habit loop, this one being writing. I do have the luxury of owning my schedule, so I can reconfigure things as necessary, but even if you don't have that privilege, there are always sacrifices and decisions you can make to incorporate whatever change you want to make happen in your life.

Another important point to recognize is that life happens, and I can't always do the things I've planned. Sometimes, there's an early meeting or phone call that changes my schedule and makes it impossible for me to write in the morning before I go to work. That's why it's important to focus on what you're trying to accomplish in the big picture and not just focus on the letter of the law. For example, I've had days where I've had all the time in the world and have written for two hours straight. And then there have been those mornings where I haven't been able concentrate, and nothing has flowed, and I've struggled through a painful ten minutes of writing.

Your practice session won't be the same every day. Some days it will come easily, and some days will be hard. I have some tips and tricks I've used on those hard days to push through (we'll get to those later), but the most important thing to do is this: at the end of each day, ask yourself if you were intentional, present, and sincere in your efforts to complete your practice that day—and if you were, congratulate yourself on another session well done, and get ready to come back again tomorrow even better and stronger.

I believe that no matter what your goal is, you can make progress every day just by getting out there and doing what you've set out to do every day. That is the definition of practice, right? Mastery over time. Daily goals allow you to make progress as well. You can break down your overall goal by setting smaller targets to achieve each day. Start very small, and then increase them as you progress with your practice. You may start off slow and hesitant, but each day, week, and month you practice you'll get better, stronger, and more comfortable. You'll progress; you'll make change happen.

Doing something every day also adds a nice simplicity to the process, in that you don't need to remember if you've done your practice two or three times this week. You don't need a complicated matrix of a schedule to track on and off days; all you need to know you're on track is a simple daily calendar.

By doing a little bit each day, you can get a lot accomplished.

TIME

Have you ever really thought how much time is in one day? It's twenty-four hours, or 1,440 minutes, or 86,400 seconds. When we aren't spending that time watching television, scrolling through Instagram, Snapchat, or Facebook, or generally wasting it on other things, we can get a lot accomplished—especially when we have a realistic sense of how long things actually take. Twenty-four hours may not seem like a lot of time, but when you're aware of how you're spending that time and are present in each moment, one day can become a goldmine.

I have to admit, I'm a stickler about time. In high school I had such a busy schedule—between taking AP classes and working twenty hours a week—that I scheduled myself down to the minute. My schedule often looked something like this: *Wake up at 5:00. Pee from 5:00–5:03. Rest two minutes. Start calculus homework at 5:05.*

As crazy as it sounds, for the most part I stuck to

that schedule. I had to if I wanted to do well in school and get into a good college. There was no way my father was going to pay for college, so I had to get good grades for scholarships and work hard at my job to save money. Fear and desire drove my early discipline. When I got to college, though, I found myself becoming less rigid. I think that was a good thing overall, but I also lost a lot of my self-discipline. Now my schedule wasn't down to the minute, or even the hour; it was more like, *Try and write that paper at some point today.* And even then I knew there would not be real consequences if I didn't accomplish my task in the allotted time frame. I mean, I would get it done eventually, right? The structure was gone because my circumstances were different. The fear and desire were gone. I didn't have to be such a stickler for time anymore, and because of that, my awareness of it diminished.

When you actually have an awareness of how long things take, your view of the day and what can be accomplished in it changes. When you say you'll be there in five minutes but you know you need to find your shoes, use the bathroom, and turn off the heater all before you even leave the house, your five minutes is actually more like ten minutes plus. A daily intentional practice that you know will take you an hour each day is great—but do you have an hour each day to spare?

If you really look at your schedule, I think you'll find that you do. But that's where the hard work comes in.

Remember, if you want different results, you have to do something different. So, how do you find that hour each day? Start by looking at your existing commitments and then finding ways to structure your time differently. For example, I'm headed to dinner and a play with a friend tonight. I know I will be tired when I get back late this evening. So I'm going to do my daily reading now, in the afternoon. Not because I have to, but because I want to. Because I know it will make me happy and fulfilled and engaged. I know it will entertain me, and I don't want to miss out on the great story I'm reading because I didn't take the time to think my day through and plan a little. I don't want to be upset later when I'm home and wanting to read, but also extremely tired. So I'm being aware, thoughtful, and honest with myself in order to make the time to do the things I want to do. I'm choosing different actions to get different results.

Time can be your best friend or your worst enemy. How aware and intentional you are with it is your call.

I've always been introspective, often asking myself questions and trying to learn more about who I am and why I do the things I do. I'm always thinking I could (and sometimes should) do better, so understanding who I am and what that means, and how it affects what I do, is a good place to start. If you're familiar with Myers Briggs Type Indicator, I am an INTJ, which means I am

Introverted, Intuitive, Thinking, and Judging. Taken together, this means I recharge my energy by being alone versus being with others. I take in information using my intuition or gut, but make decisions using rational thinking rather than my feelings. And lastly, I orient to the world based on judgment, not perception.

The INTJ profile is often described as "The Mastermind" or "The Architect," according to 16Personalities, a website that outlines the sixteen combinations of the four aspects of the Myers Briggs Type Indicator. Of the Architect they say, "People with the INTJ personality type are imaginative yet decisive, ambitious yet private, amazingly curious, but they do not squander their energy." This describes me pretty accurately in a lot of different ways. One of my fears of writing this book is the potential of losing my privacy, but my desire to share my story with others who may take something positive from it pushes me forward.

As part of my curiosity about myself, I like to measure things—not just for fun but in order to determine what I want to improve and whether progress is being made. An old boss of my mine used to say that if something can be measured, it can be improved. There are certainly ways to take this idea too far, but when it comes to individual improvement, it's a pretty good approach. Changing a habit is hard for me, just as it is for everyone, but I've fully embraced the mantra of, *Nothing changes if nothing changes.* This is why I dedicate myself to personal growth through my daily intentional practice each year.

At the beginning of this year, a friend of mine wrote a Facebook post about getting rid of New Year's resolutions and calling them "Annual Indulgences" instead.

His desire was to *indulge* in more time at the gym. To *indulge* in healthy, delicious food.

I love this approach for a couple reasons. First, my friend is taking a positive approach and using language that elicits feelings of joy versus pain. Who doesn't want to indulge in fun things? It sounds decadent and maybe even a little naughty and a lot better than depriving yourself. And if you're indulging in things that are good for you, all the better.

Second, my friend's approach is very much in line with the idea I've been talking about: addition versus subtraction. Remember, whether you're calling what you're doing intentions or indulgences, the idea is to think about what you're *adding* to your life, not what you're taking away. This is not about quitting something; it's not about subtracting or withholding something from yourself. This practice is about what you're doing to augment your life, what you're going to indulge in, how you're going to grow. If you want to quit smoking, what routine are you going to add to your life to replace the cigarette with something else, something positive? What gift are you going to give yourself this year? This month? Today? This moment?

Happiness is not in the future. It's not tomorrow or next week. It's right now. The future never comes; we're always in the present moment. So don't wait for the start of a new year or new month to start adding to your life. Every day, every moment, we have a chance for a brand-new beginning. What are you going to do with yours? We can talk about how we want things to be. We can dream. But what if we actually *did* something? What if, a year from now, your life was different? *You* were different? All because you stopped and thought about how you were spending your time? Because you were aware and intentional and committed yourself to adding something to your life through a daily practice, and then you actually did it?

Your change can be something small or big; it can be something you just do for that one year, or for the rest of your life. Wherever you take it, it starts by being intentional in your practice each and every day, starting with today. Remember, nothing changes if nothing changes.

3.
The Beginning

HOPEFULLY BY NOW I'VE CONVINCED YOU THAT CHANGE IS POSSIBLE WITH A DAILY INTENTIONAL PRACTICE. AND HOPEFULLY YOU WANT TO HEAR MORE ABOUT MY SEVEN years of practicing every day and what I've learned along the way. Not every year has created a new habit that's stuck around after the end of the year, but I've definitely learned something with every new practice that has made each subsequent year that much easier. I sometimes think about where I would be now if I could go back and apply those lessons to my practices from the beginning. My hope is that you will be able to take the benefit of those lessons as you start your own intentional practice.

People often ask me how I got started on my daily practice journey. Truth be told, this all started as an afterthought. Looking back now, it was a pretty meaningful afterthought, but it certainly wasn't something I planned. In fact, the first year was probably so much fun because it was an accident. I really did not set out to work out every day of my life for a year. I didn't even set out to work out every day for a month. Honestly, I was just getting up and doing what I felt.

It was sometime in the fall of 2010 when I looked up and realized that I had been working out every day for a while. I looked at my calendar and tried to figure out how long I'd gone without a break or a day off. Because I hadn't been tracking it, I didn't know the answer, and that really bugged me. So I asked myself, *What would happen if I tried to do it intentionally? Would I be able to commit to exercising every single day for one year?* The following year, I set out to see if I could do it.

THE OTHER BEGINNING

Although I played sports in high school, I never really thought of myself as an athlete. I was a decent enough soccer player and could defend pretty well on the basketball court, though I couldn't make a shot if you paid me. In college I didn't play any sports outside of a semester rowing overseas when I studied at Oxford University. And when I realized I would never be tall enough to be a very good rower, I took up Shotokan karate instead.

While I enjoyed karate and rowing, it was more the

social aspects of those activities that I really liked, not the movement itself. It was a chance to get to meet other students studying at Oxford and to build relationships more easily. I was part of the Oxford karate team that made history by finally ending Cambridge's winning streak over us at our annual match, and celebrating with team in the pub afterwards was an amazing experience I'll never forget. Although I hadn't done much to secure the win, I felt part of something special that night. I felt good not because of anything I had done physically, but because of the camaraderie and social connections my involvement in the team had brought me.

I kept up with karate for a bit when I returned to school in California, but like most things in my life at that point, I couldn't make it stick. I didn't have the same social connection with the karate dojo (gym) back in California, and I wasn't very interested in doing things that were hard at the time. And karate was hard.

I've read a number of articles that talk about how people born under the Aries zodiac sign get excited easily about things, but can't finish anything. I don't know if that's true, but I do know that I tend to think a lot of things are really great ideas at first and jump into them—and then I have a hard time following through and finishing what I started. I often end up quitting after barely getting started.

I also used to be that way about people. You know, you meet someone new and they seem great at first;

then you get to know them over time and the shine comes off. I'm not sure if that's an Aries trait or just who I was, but an honest assessment of my behavior in past years would show that I treated both the people and the activities in my life this way. You could look in my closet to see the money I wasted on equipment and clothes for activities I tried once or twice and did initially love, but never went back to.

After karate I really didn't do anything else sports related until my first round of losing a lot of weight. Like I said before, I've struggled with my weight most of my life. I wasn't really a fat or chunky kid, but growing up I felt bigger than I wanted to be. Looking back now, I realize that I wasn't heavy at all, I just wasn't a small stick like a lot of the skinny girls I went to school with. As I got older and puberty came around I did get bigger and was probably carrying twenty more pounds than I wanted when I went to college. And aside from my brief Oxford Blues stint and my introduction to Shotokan Karate, I was pretty sedentary during college.

After graduation, when I started working in the real world as a legal assistant, is when things really took a turn for the worse. I gained another twenty pounds, and could easily have been called fat (if you were so rudely inclined). Working in an office all day, sitting at desk with very little movement and the worst type of foods easily available, is a quick recipe to weight gain.

Add to that the stress of not liking your job and you're easily looking at tight pants, blouses that no longer fit, and eating McDonald's at ten o'clock at night to make yourself feel better—even though you know that won't make you feel better at all. When you're on that hamster wheel it's hard to stop falling prey to your bad habits, and even harder to recognize what you're doing sometimes.

Like I said before, the first time I lost the weight was when I was living in Los Angeles. I had my wisdom teeth extracted and couldn't eat for a couple days; that's what jumpstarted my weight loss efforts. After that, I basically just stopped eating and started working out all the time—at least an hour in the morning and an hour later in the day.

The good news is, I lost the weight. The bad news is, I quickly gained it back when a cute girl didn't call me back. Yep, something as simple as a lack of a phone call from a stranger was enough to shake my self-confidence and send me back into a downward spiral.

During that time, I never really enjoyed working out. Exercise was simply a means to an end, and that end was to be "skinny" and get a date. It was definitely not the right approach, and while I initially got the results I thought I wanted, being skinny, it was pretty much guaranteed from the start that the long-term results would not be there.

WHAT'S YOUR WHY?

It took me a while to recognize my first mistake. Doing things for the wrong reasons rarely gets you the right results in the long term. If you truly want long-lasting results, you have to start with your long-term goal in mind and focus on the true reason you're doing something.

I finally lost the weight for good when I decided I wanted to be healthy and do the things I had dreamed of for a while. When I focused on that as my why, and not on being skinny, I knew that lasting change was going happen.

It was 2001 and my twenty-eighth birthday was coming up; I was getting old. (Yes, back then I thought thirty was old. How I long for those days now.) I thought if I changed a few small things in my life, I could accomplish anything. So, when I turned twenty-eight, I made a list of things to do before I turned thirty. (Yep, I'm one of those people: a list maker. We'll get back to that later.)

My list of things to accomplish before I turned thirty was designed to remind me that I was still young and to give me a sense of accomplishment. I wanted to learn to play the guitar, ask someone out (can you believe I'd never officially done that before?), run a marathon, and complete a triathlon.

Keep in mind, this was a list made by someone who didn't know how to swim and couldn't run a mile without stopping. So why a marathon and a triathlon? Because I had watched the 1997 Ironman World Championship on NBC, when Sian Welch and Wendy Ingraham gave everything they had as they crawled to the finish line in a battle for fourth place. Can you imagine that? With nothing left in you and the championship already claimed, you literally crawl on your hands and knees to get to the finish line?

That sense of accomplishment, of strength, of never giving up, resonated with me. Those women's ability to push through the tough times appealed to me on a visceral level, and I wanted that feeling for myself. I thought accomplishing these physical feats would give me that feeling and allow me to translate it to other parts of my life. I was scared when I wrote down "complete a triathlon" without knowing how to swim, but I also knew that I needed to do it.

Making my "Things To Do Before Thirty" list was exactly what I needed to jumpstart me to get moving. I wasn't thinking about getting skinny, I was just focused on completing my list. I like goals, and even more, I like *meeting* my goals. Just writing out the list made me feeling younger, and starting to work on them in the smallest of ways only increased that feeling. That was my *why*, and it's important to remember that the *why* started with a focus on joy and accomplishment for myself and not because of someone else.

BUILDING BLOCKS

So, if I was going to run a marathon, I needed to get started running, right? Trust me when I say that even the *thought* of starting to run was intimidating to me at the time. When I first got out there I couldn't run for more than a minute at a time. Yes, after one minute of running I was wiped. I had to stop and gather myself, catch my breath, shake out my legs, and then I could get going again.

I quickly discovered the joy of a walk/run training program, and I slowly increased from one minute, to two minutes, to three minutes of running, and then a one-minute walk before returning to a run. I slowly increased my run minutes each week, and the day I ran thirty minutes without stopping I actually cried. I might have been crying because I was exhausted, but it also felt like tears of joy and success and accomplishment. I had done it—I had run thirty minutes without stopping. It was something that had seemed impossible just a month earlier, and now it was real.

That little bit of success gave me the boost I needed to know that I could accomplish much more—maybe even all of the goals on my list. It was a small win, an important part of successful change initiatives as I discussed earlier and will go into more detail about later. I was starting to build a foundation of achievement that would lead to more accomplishments later.

MORE BLOCKS TO PLAY WITH

After getting a little bit of success with running, I knew I needed to start tackling the other parts of a triathlon, the swim and the bike. A couple points of clarification, since when most people think of triathlons, they think about the Ironman World Championships in Hawaii. That's the one you see on TV, with people sometimes crawling to the finish line but always exuberant when they complete the race. That's the big enchilada of triathlons: a 2.4-mile swim, 112-mile bike, and a marathon of 26.2 miles, all covered in one day. It's like the Super Bowl of triathlons; the very best athletes in various age groups compete in this race.

This is not the triathlon I was going to do. There are several other standard triathlon distances. One is the half Ironman, which is exactly what it sounds like: participants do half of the distances listed above. Then there's the standard Olympic or international distance triathlon, which is what's raced at the Olympic games and internationally. It is approximately half of the distances of the half Ironman. Finally, there's the sprint triathlon—the shortest one—which consists of a half-mile swim, 12.4-mile bike, and 3.1-mile run. That may not sound like a lot, but for someone who had just started running thirty minutes straight, didn't know how to swim, and hadn't been on a bike in years, those distances seemed impossible to me.

Not only did I not know how to swim, I was terrified

of water; I had no business thinking about swimming anything, much less spending my hard-earned dollars to pay for a race where I was probably going to drown. But that's exactly what I did when I signed up for the Treasure Island Sprint Triathlon in 2001. I honestly did not know how I was going to learn to swim before the race, but I was determined to do it. And when I'm determined to do something I can be a stubborn you-know-what. I was counting on my ability to be relentless.

Lucky for me, I was a member of the Embarcadero YMCA at the time. They had a women's triathlon club that offered beginning triathlon training programs, as well as coaches and other athletes to train with. The women were friendly and kind, and a number of them were also in the same position I was: they were triathlon novices. We were all looking to change our lives in big and small ways for a number of different reasons. Some of us were getting older and wanted to stop the passage of time; some were coming off of heartbreak and looking to put their energy into something positive. Regardless of our individual situation, we were all seeking change, and having a group to learn and train with was what we needed. We also had amazing coaches who taught us everything about racing triathlons and made our goals that much more accessible and fun.

But first, I had to learn how to swim.

BLACK PEOPLE DON'T SWIM

The first time I got in the swimming pool, Head Coach Shannon asked me to "give her fifty." I had no idea what she meant. Did she want fifty dollars, fifty pushups, fifty laps? It took me a moment or two to realize she meant she wanted me to swim the fifty meters of the pool—down to the other end and back. That's how out of my element I was.

Reluctantly, I stuck my head in the water and paddled as hard as I could, kicking my legs and moving my arms in what I thought was a swimming motion. A while later, certain I'd made it to the other end of the pool and it was time to turn around, I stood up and looked around. Imagine my surprise and disappointment when I realized I was only ten feet away . . . *from the wall I had started from*. I hadn't gone anywhere. All that effort, and I had barely moved in the water. I could have walked that distance faster. That was my swimming starting point.

Coach Shannon laughed quietly when she realized what she had to work with. Sure, this was a beginning swimming class, but everyone else had at least some sense of what they were doing in the water. Most of them were really only there to improve their technique; they weren't grown adults that couldn't swim a lick. I was the only true beginner.

I hated to be yet another stereotype, but I was indeed a black person who not only didn't know how to swim but was scared of the water. I was the only black woman in the pool, and although I definitely felt a sense of otherness, I also felt empathy and encouragement from everyone else. There were other women in the program who were fish in the water but struggled with running, or the bike, or transitioning from one discipline to another. I learned that everyone had something they were working on, and together we could help each other improve in our particular areas of weakness.

The day of the triathlon came approximately two months after the September 11 terrorist attacks in the United States. The race was being held on Treasure Island, which sits between Oakland and San Francisco, butted up against the Bay Bridge. Because of the terrorist attacks, there were security concerns around the bridge, so at the very last minute, the race organizers changed the bike course. Athletes who had actually trained on Treasure Island prior to the race— me included—had to adapt to a new course on the fly.

I was so worried about getting through the swim that I put the bike changes out of my mind as I put on my wetsuit and wandered closer to the water with the other athletes. I was scared and excited and wondering what the heck made me think this was a good idea.

THE PLAN GOES AWRY

When the race announcer called us to the start, we all waded into the bay and started treading water until the starting gun went off. I tried to remember everything Coach Shannon and the rest of the YMCA Women's Triathlon team and coaches had taught me. When the gun went off I put my head in the water, lifted my hips, and extended my arm for my first stroke—and *BAM*, I got kicked in the head. The swimmer in front of me had extended her legs and caught the side of my head, causing me to lose position and start to turn over.

Everything I learned in training went out the window, and for a second I thought I was dying. *I knew this wasn't a good idea*, I thought. Then I flashed back to a swim session where we practiced swimming over each other—yes, we actually climbed on top of other athletes in the water to prepare for this exact moment—and that's when my preparation kicked in, pun intended, and all my practice made a difference. I took a moment to regroup, took a deep breath, and looked around. I found my land markers, and I started off again on the swim. All of the little tips, tricks, and tools I'd learned in training and during practice sessions came back to me, and I made it through the swim. My practice paid off in ways I couldn't have imagined all those mornings in the pool and it may even have saved my life that morning.

I was elated that I not only survived the swim leg, I completed it—and I wasn't even the last person out of the water. After taking way too long in the transition to peel off my wetsuit and refuel, next up was the new bike course and whatever fresh challenges that held. I pushed through the confusion and anxiety I felt over the course change and tried to call upon my swim success to pull me through.

I was physically and mentally exhausted when I got off my bike, and again questioned every choice that had gotten me to this moment. I was tired, in pain, and wanted to stop—but I also knew I had more in me. I remembered every time I had quit something before, only to realize afterwards I could have pushed through and finished. I didn't want this to be one of those times. I made a promise to myself: Even if it meant crawling my way in, I was going to finish this damn race.

I tried to start off running, but my legs were dead coming off the bike, so it was more of a shuffle until they loosened up and I could actually run. I was reduced to walking again about two miles in. I started seeing visions, but I knew I was going to make it, no matter what. Something had shifted in me and I could feel it. I had moved from having hope that I could finish to a quiet certainty that I would—that I was going to do it, no matter what. I believed, and that was the key to finishing.

That final stretch on the run, when I could see my friends cheering for me and the look of pride and love on their faces, was beyond anything I had imagined during those hours and hours of practice. Knowing that for once in my life I hadn't quit something, that I was finally a finisher, was priceless. It was a spectacular, overwhelming experience, and I was officially addicted—not just to triathlons and exercise, but to finishing things I started. I was a "completer" now, and I knew I could do anything I set my mind to.

I went on to do other triathlons, and eventually transitioned to marathons over the years. I successfully did my first full marathon before my thirtieth birthday, and went on to do four others in the years that followed. Ultimately, just doing the things I loved jumpstarted my weight loss, and that has enabled me to keep my weight in check over the years.

This experience taught me a number of valuable lessons that I would go on to apply to my daily intentional practice a few years later, though I didn't know it at the time. Losing the weight this second time—the right way and for the right reasons—set me on a course that changed my life. I found that I loved sweating. I loved moving my body and seeing the changes that came from it. I loved asking my body and mind to do difficult things and having the mental strength to accomplish them. I loved training every day (otherwise known as practicing). I became a fitness addict by accidentally creating a habit.

I worked out consistently during those years after my

first triathlon, but when I "just didn't feel like it," I didn't do it. Sometimes I wanted to sleep in, so I did. *What's the big deal?* I'd ask myself. *I already lost the weight and figured out how to keep it off, so who cares if I miss a day here and there, right?*

That's the question I tried to answer with my first year of daily practice. Could I push through those days when I just didn't feel like it? Could I not have a missed day here and there? That first year of my daily intentional practice was about making working out a consistent habit by not letting a day slip away because I was tired or feeling lazy. It was about seeing if I could make consistency a goal—which, for me, was relatively easy, since it was already something I was naturally drawn to. I had learned that I like to work out. I like to sweat. For someone who doesn't like these things, working out might be a really hard thing to start with. One of the best ways to create consistency is to make it easy on yourself from the beginning. As you think about creating your own daily practice, focus on starting with something you like and are naturally drawn to.

Starting with the right "why" can also make all the difference in the world. What's your why? Ralph Waldo Emerson said, "A foolish consistency is the hobgoblin of little minds," and he was right when it comes to uniformity for the sake of conformity. The goal is definitely not foolish consistency; rather, it's a thoughtful and aware consistency, one created through intentionally practicing what you love on a daily basis.

4.

Vegetables Are Scary Things

GREAT, I DID IT. I ACCOMPLISHED MY GOAL OF AT LEAST
THIRTY MINUTES OF CARDIO EVERY DAY FOR ONE YEAR. SO,
WHAT WOULD COME NEXT?

I wanted to keep going but knew I didn't want to
keep working out as my daily practice. I needed to try
something new and different, and I wanted to keep
challenging myself. I enjoyed the high of meeting a
goal, of accomplishing something I set out to do, and
I wanted to see if I could keep it going. I was deep into
the virtuous reward cycle that Duhigg talks about in *The
Power of Habit.*

As I mentioned before, Duhigg's theory of habit
creation and change involves a cycle of cue, reward,
and routine. Now that I had a routine that provided the
reward I desired, I wanted to keep getting that reward. I
had started achieving my goals and was in the "virtuous

reward cycle," and I wanted to keep it going; that feeling of success itself had also become a habit, and one I wasn't ready to give up just yet. When you accomplish something you've set out to do, it's like getting a runner's high—a flood of endorphins. I wanted more.

WHAT COMES NEXT

I knew working out was not the right daily practice for my next year of daily intentional practice for three reasons: 1) you need to rest the body sometimes; 2) working out was already something I had made a habit and was doing consistently, so it was no longer a challenge; and 3) there were other things I wanted to work on—other things I needed to add to my life.

Not everyone will feel this way. Maybe your first daily practice won't go as well as you'd hoped, and you'll want to continue it. It's okay to try a daily practice again. I do recommend, however, that you do it with a slightly different practice goal or even over a different time period. Remember, the goal is to do it consistently and daily, but you can change any of the other elements as necessary.

Anyway, in my case, it was clearly time to move on to something new. Since I had started with something I loved, I thought about tackling something I definitely did not enjoy next. Something that for sure wasn't a habit and probably would never be one for me. I decided to focus on eating vegetables.

STINKY VEGETABLES

I've got to be honest with you, I've always hated vegetables. Always. I was that kid who tried to hide her them in her napkin at dinner. If we'd had a family dog, you can be certain that dog would have been eating its weight in the green stuff every night. And while I don't hate *all* vegetables, I disliked enough of them to brand the whole group as disgusting.

I know, I know, I'm an adult and I should have let it go a long time ago, but I have this weird thing about not eating or drinking things that don't taste good to me. It's the same reason I don't drink: I can't stand the taste of alcohol. I know that if I kept at it, the taste would dull—but why would I do that? I've never understood the notion of continuing to put something in your mouth that you just don't like. Alcohol is just not my thing and never has been. Same with vegetables.

And the thought of eating them—no. I did *not* want to do this as my daily practice. I mean, kicking and screaming, I did not want to do it. And not just because I didn't like most vegetables and it would be a year of eating things I didn't like; the bigger reason was that it scared the crap out of me.

When I started working out every day, it sounded like a *fun* challenge—something I could get into as I tackled it. But eating one serving of vegetables every day for a year certainly did not sound fun in any way, shape, or form. No, it sounded scary. It sounded like inevitable failure. And I wasn't ready for failure again—not now that I had tasted success. But I knew part of the challenge was to do things that I feared and that would help me grow, and as much as I was kicking and screaming, I knew in my heart that a daily vegetable practice was the right one for me at that time. It was the year before I turned forty, and I told myself it was finally time to grow up and try to eat like a healthy adult.

CONQUERING THE FEAR

I started the year with apprehension, but also some excitement carrying over from my success the previous year. I didn't really have a plan, other than to eat one serving of vegetables, at some point, every day.

The first few days of the year were okay, with me sticking pretty much to the vegetables I knew and liked, including carrots, broccoli, and my favorite, okra. But after a few weeks I was starting to get tired of just eating those three foods—and worse, I was starting to forget about my daily practice until later in the day. There were several nights in January and February when I pulled myself out of bed at ten o'clock at night to shove some broccoli in my mouth. And then, of course, I had to go brush my teeth again, and I ended up going to bed grumpy and annoyed with myself, and with a gross, toothpaste-plus-vegetable taste in my mouth.

It took me a while, but I finally started to figure out how to make this practice work. First, I realized that I had to incorporate it into my daily life in a more manageable way every day, so I sat down and thought about my schedule. How and when did I eat throughout the day? Just like with all daily intentional practices, it all had to start with awareness. The first step is always to examine my life truthfully and be brutally honest and accurate with myself about what I'm currently doing and what I can realistically do differently in my life. The awareness moment is not the time to lie to yourself or "hope and pray" things can be different. It is a time for frankness and honesty with yourself.

MAKING IT WORK

Back then I was eating oatmeal for breakfast and rarely ate dinner, so it made the most sense to try to tackle my vegetables at lunch. By looking at my schedule realistically and committing myself to a time of the day for my practice, I helped ensure that I was at least giving myself a fighting chance to be successful.

The next step was realizing that I couldn't do this one by myself. My lifelong dislike of vegetables had also caused me to be pretty ignorant about them; I needed input from other people. So I started asking friends for suggestions of different options, hoping to expand my knowledge beyond the three vegetables I had been eating.

Again, without realizing it, I was actually incorporating one of the key elements of a successful daily intentional practice—first, by finding ways to adjust my life to meet the goal rather than trying to go with an all-or-none approach, and second, by telling others and getting support.

By the summer, I was on track with my daily practice, and I had even learned I liked a few new vegetables, including eggplant and Brussels sprouts. Coworkers and friends were checking in with me and asking what vegetables I had eaten that day, encouraging me to continue when I was feeling done with it, and making helpful suggestions about new vegetables to try or new ways to cook ones I was already familiar with. What I thought was going to be a terrible experience turned into a pretty good one. No, I didn't end up loving vegetables and no, I definitely don't eat them every day these days, but I do certainly eat more than I did before, and I've expanded the range of vegetables I like and eat. And that wouldn't have happened if I hadn't done this thing that scared me a little.

What are the things that scare you? Is there a way you can add them to your life? Remember, it doesn't have to be something huge; if you're afraid of heights, you don't have to jump out of a plane. You can start with something small, like going to top of your building and looking out every day for two minutes. If you live in Chicago, go to the top of Sears Tower (or whatever they're calling it now) and look out every day, or go to the tallest publicly accessible building in your town. Just trying something that scares you a little is a great starting place. Push yourself; it will be worth it. And if you can push yourself every day, you will not only make it a habit, you will likely also conquer a fear in the process. As I learned from my daily intentional vegetable practice, doing something that scares you a little can pay off a lot.

Brené Brown recently wrote a post online about the three questions she asks herself at the end of the year as she looks to the start of a new year. Brown is the author of *Daring Greatly*, *Rising Strong*, *Braving The Wilderness*, and numerous other bestselling books, and she's someone whose work I really love and resonate with. I love her idea of asking ourselves questions at certain intervals, because they prompt us to take stock in a deeper and more meaningful way than we usually do. I particularly like the questions she asks, because they all focus around the idea of exploring what you can add to your life. Her questions are:

1. What do I want more of in my life?
2. How do I let go of what's no longer serving me?
3. What will make me feel more alive? Braver?

Note that she asks the specific question of what will make her *braver* in addition to what will make her feel more alive. If you're struggling to find what your daily intentional practice should be, start by asking yourself modified versions of Brown's three questions. What do you want to add to your life in a sustainable way? What can you change about the things that are not serving you? What will make you feel alive and scares you a little? This is a great starting point for determining what would be your appropriate daily intentional practice.

5.
Full-Ass Mantras

IT WAS DIFFICULT, BUT I GOT THROUGH THAT YEAR OF VEGGIES. AND WHEN I DID, AGAIN I ASKED MYSELF, *What's next?*

I had continued working out pretty consistently during my year of vegetables, but rarely, if ever, did I stretch. Add to that the previous year of working out 365 days in a row, and you know my joints and muscles were aching. So, in 2013, I decided my daily intentional practice would be to stretch every day.

I have to admit, this was probably the weakest goal I've created in my journey thus far. But frankly, after that tough year of vegetables, I wanted something easier to tackle next. Stretching was something I needed to do that would add to my life, and I knew this was one physical improvement I needed to work on that I probably wouldn't improve without making a specific effort and intention to do so.

HALF-ASSING IT

While stretching has turned out to be the weakest daily practice I've taken on, it's also the practice that taught me one of my most valuable lessons: in choosing something "easy," I unintentionally set myself up to half-ass my daily intentional practice for the year.

What does it mean to "half-ass" your practice? You know when you're a kid and someone makes you pick up your toys, or apologize to another kid for something, and although you're technically *doing it*, everything about your demeanor and energy is saying that you're not? When you're dragging your feet and barely making eye contact—that's half-assing it.

Don't let yourself do this with your daily intentional practice. Commit to something you actually really want, that will challenge and scare you a little but make you feel good in the end, because if you don't, you may end up half-assing it. That's what happened to me with stretching: While I did stretch each day, the extent to which I did it, and how much time, energy, and effort I put into it overall, was pretty pathetic. Because it was something I "kinda" wanted, I "kinda" did it. Don't waste your time doing that.

My first mistake was not setting a clear enough intention for the year. As with every time you set out to practice, it starts with awareness, and I didn't have it that year. The farthest I got in terms of thinking about it was, *I should be stretching more, so I guess I'll stretch.*

I didn't set a specific goal, like "stretch for X period of time," or "do these five stretches every day," or any other type of structure that would have helped me focus on what I was really trying to practice. I simply said I would stretch. So, instead of being enamored and a little scared of the practice, as I had been my first two years, I kind of knew going in that it would be easy. I could phone my practice in if I really needed to. My heart and soul weren't in it.

If I had been more aware and brutally honest with myself in the beginning, I would have known this and admitted it to myself. Instead, I felt more obligated to practice than excited for the opportunity to do it each day. I did it so I could check the box, but that was about all I did—which led to one of my favorite mantras that I've used every year since then: "Don't Check the Box, Own the Box."

MANTRAS FOR THE WIN

Using mantras for your daily practice can help you own the box. Each year I start by writing down a mantra for the year in front of the same calendar I use to track my daily intentional practice. Two of the several definitions of mantras include: 1) a sound, word, or phrase that is repeated by someone who is praying or meditating; and 2) a word or phrase that is repeated often or that expresses someone's basic beliefs. While my use of mantras is not quite like praying or meditating, I do often repeat them as a guide throughout the year to remind myself of what I'm trying to do or where I'm trying to go. Some of the mantras I've used in the past few years include "Bear Down and Be Proud" and "Only You Can Make You Happy." Even saying these words now remind me of the lessons I needed to learn or the message I wanted to ingrain in myself each of those years.

"Bear Down and Be Proud" was my mantra for 2011, when I was in my last year of graduate school and working at a very busy job. I knew it was going to be an extremely busy year and likely pretty tough to get through. Setting the expectation in the beginning that it was going to be a challenging year, and reminding myself that in the end I was going to be proud of my hard work, helped me get through it. "Only You Can Make You Happy," meanwhile, was a reminder to stop looking to other people to "complete" me or make me happy, versus taking control of what I wanted and finding ways to make myself happy on my own.

YOUR MANTRA

If you find it difficult to practice a daily intention that you haven't fully embraced yet, one mantra that might be helpful is "Ritualize to Actualize." You make something a ritual for yourself by actually doing it. And when you do something every day, it becomes a habit or ritual—"Actualize to Ritualize." It works both ways and can be repeated both ways.

When we honor our word to ourselves we become more committed, intentional, and decisive with what we're trying to accomplish. The more you do it the more you will believe you *can* do it, which will have you doing it more. It is a cycle that starts by believing from the very beginning that you can, and will, and then setting that belief into action. All it takes is one action. Not talking about what you're going to do anymore but actually *doing* something about it. And like I said earlier, you can start small, with a tiny victory, then build on it and go from there.

Why are mantras so important to me that I have both annual ones and different ones I use as part of my daily intentional practice? Because I started using them when I was training for my first marathon, and I saw the benefits immediately. I'm not sure where they came from, or even how it began, but it was during that time that I started repeating words to myself—when I was on long training runs. Those words got me through some difficult moments during tough training sessions.

The core of any marathon training program is the long run. At least once a week, you have to get out there and put feet to pavement (or treadmill). You can run for miles or for time, but if you want to make it 26.2 miles, you've simply got to put in the mileage. It doesn't matter how fast or how slow you go, you've just got to keep going, step after step. And let me tell you, those steps can get pretty long, boring, and hard after a while.

Even listening to music gets old when you're on mile sixteen and your big toe is hurting and your shoulder feels weird and you think you're not going to make it.

What helps then is a reminder of why you're out there. Why you've made this commitment to yourself. Because you want to run a marathon. Because it will mean that you're young again, or capable of setting goals and meeting them, or are fit and healthy. Or that you're not someone that has great ideas that fizzle out, or someone that quits things. Or that you're strong, or everything or anything you want to be. Maybe it means nothing at all—but you're out there now and you've got miles to go, so what do you do?

This is where mantras come in. The ability to remind yourself, especially during the hard times, why you're doing what you're doing, is so very important. I've had all sorts of strange and funny mantras over the year. When I was racing the one I focused on was often "Pain Is Temporary, Glory Is Forever." A friend told me his was "Pain Is Temporary, Web Results Are Forever." For him, being able to look up his race results online was his driving motivation. That wasn't as important for me. Competing with others was never my thing. Competing with myself was more than enough for me. To know that I would have the glory of finishing the race forever and no one could take it away from me—that was my motivation.

Other mantras that have been useful to me mid-race

include a reminder of all the delicious food I'm going to eat afterwards. In fact, toward the end of the Chicago Marathon in 2005, I remember running up to a couple women who were going back and forth naming all the food they were going to eat after the race, including burritos, pizza, and fried chicken. I added donuts and ice cream to their list because as I mentioned earlier, sweets and sugar are my weaknesses. We chatted for a few blocks, and then I ran on to get my ceremonial post-race Dunkin Donuts Bavarian Creme.

Having different phrases that remind you why you're doing what you're doing doesn't just apply to running and marathons. As I mentioned, I use mantras as I start each new year of life. Again, when I was working full time and in graduate school, my mantra for the year was "Bear Down, Be Proud." When I didn't want to finish my reading for the week or write that paper, I would go back and read those words to myself and do just that—bear down and get to work—so I could eventually be proud. Saying those four words out loud to myself was enough to remind me of the bigger goal, reorient myself, and get me going again.

The mantra I adopted the year after getting my master's was "Have Fun," because I had earned it and I knew I needed it. Short, sweet, simple, and to the point—that was all that was necessary. Mantras don't have to always be tough. My mantra for this year, for example, is "Do the Things that Make You Happy." Why?

Because I realized that I spend a lot of time working, and not nearly enough time doing the things I actually love—the things that bring me happiness and joy. So I wrote it down where I could see it in the front of my calendar, and I repeat it to myself often.

Joe Madden, Manager for the 2016 World Series Champions Chicago Cubs, uses mantras to encourage and motivate his teams as well. Their mantra their championship year was "Embrace the Target," because he knew with all the pieces he had assembled they were the favored team, and although they hadn't won anything yet, they were expected to perform. Sometimes people and teams shrink from that kind of pressure and expectation, but Madden made it clear that they were not only going to talk about it, they were going embrace it and make it their own.

When things got tough and the Cubs lost multiple games in a row, that mantra served as a touchstone that everyone could return to, something to remind them why they were doing drills in the morning, why they were still working on batting practice when their arms were tired, why they were still practicing fielding late into the day. And the following season, Madden's new mantra, "One Breath," reminded the team of how they'd won the previous year's championship: by playing as one team, one group, and by focusing on one breath at a time, one moment at a time, etc.

When I pick a mantra for the year, I try to think

about a few key words that will instantly take me back to a feeling of inspiration, hope, and yes, belief that I can actually accomplish the huge goals I've set for myself. What key words will help you get to that feeling instantly? Stop for a moment, think about the goals you want to accomplish in whatever time frame you've created for yourself, and feel the sense of possibility they inspire. What words come to mind that will help you get back to that feeling? If your goal is to walk one mile every day for the next month, maybe it's something like "One Step at a Time" or "Step by Step, I'll Get There." If your goal is to read every day, maybe your mantra is "What's the Story for Today?" or "A Few Pages to a New World." Whatever resonates with you is what you should focus on. And don't worry if it doesn't come to you right away or easily. Good mantras sometimes take time and they can't be forced. Let yours come to you as you think about the things you want to add to your life.

Lastly, I encourage you to write down your mantras. I'm old school; I used write everything down, from notes for work to things I want to say to people. I got accustomed to finding little scraps of paper with random phrases on them throughout my apartment. But if paper isn't your way, "write" using technology. Now, I often use the Notes app on my phone, for example, to jot down book recommendations from friends, restaurants I like, or just random things I come across. Whether you write it down on a piece of paper or use your computer or phone, studies have shown that writing things down helps us remember them better. And I know that writing things down has always helped me really own information at a deeper level.

The other benefit to writing down your mantras is that you can physically look at the words over and over, both as a reminder and for extra encouragement. One of my favorite shows, *Being Mary Jane*, opens with the lead character, Mary Jane Paul (portrayed by Gabrielle Union), in her bathroom, looking at a mirror with tons of Post-its with inspirational quotes and sayings from famous (and not-so-famous) people around it.

The purpose of the Post-its is to provide motivation for Mary Jane, but they're also a strong physical reminder of the things she wants to accomplish and improve upon in her life.

There's no reason why you can't do that too. It's okay to use other people's words for inspiration and encouragement. I do, however, recommend that you also use your own words, in the form of a dedicated mantra, to do the same thing. Knowing that your own words, and not just those of a famous person who's seemingly accomplished a lot, are speaking back to you can be a pretty powerful thing.

Mantras can be great and inspiring, but what to do when they don't work? When you really just don't want to do your intentional practice for the day? I'm sure you know this already, but 365 days is a long time.

A very long time. And as excited as you may be to do whatever it is you've picked, trust me when I say there will be days you don't want to do it—and days when you want to do it but feel you can't. Whether it's because you're not feeling well physically or are mentally tired and drained, there will be moments when completing whatever you've chosen will seem like the hardest thing in the world. What do you do then?

I wish I could tell you, "Don't worry about it. Take a day off, it's not that big of a deal." The voices in your head will definitely tell you that. And it will seem like they're right. But the truth is they're not. They are lying to you. They are the voices of fear and defeat. They don't want you to change and they don't believe you *can* change.

Listen to the other voices. The ones that made you believe you could do it in the first place. The voices that speak to you in the quiet moments by yourself, that dream of everything you could become. Those are the voices that are telling you the truth. They want you to succeed, and they know you have it in you to do it. This is your future self. The person you're meant to be. The person you're going to become when you truly commit to the change you want to see.

We all have a future self, and that self—whether we're talking about the parent who learns patience with their child or the struggling actor who writes herself a check for a million dollars when she's living in her car—is powerful. They want to show up and help you, but you've got to listen to that voice and not the voice of fear.

WRITE IT OUT

In addition to listening to your future self, there are a few practical things you can do to self-motivate on the days when you don't want to meet your goal.

First, go back to your list of reasons why you're doing what you're doing for this daily practice. If you haven't written that list yet, stop and write it now. Seriously, I want you to stop reading for a moment and write down the reasons why you want to change. Write down at least three, along with why you've chosen this goal for the year (or month, or whatever time frame you've settled on).

Look at the list critically and ask yourself: *Are these reasons about me and for me?* You can't change for someone else or because someone else wants you to. In order for real change to happen, it has to come from inside you, because when the days are tough and you don't think you can do it, there will only be you in the mirror. Are the three reasons you've written down your best three? You can add more than three to the list, but make sure the top three really are the most important ones to you and for you. Lastly, if you're looking back at a list you wrote earlier, are those reasons still true—do they still resonate with you?

Now that you have your list written, think about how you're going to use it when you're having a really difficult day. Know that the next time it just doesn't seem like you have it in you to complete your daily intentional practice, you'll be able to look at this list again. When you do, take it to heart; hear yourself in that moment. Then get it done. Don't think, just do. Put on your walking shoes and go. Get out your yoga mat and stretch. Take out your book and get to reading. Turn on your computer and start writing. After reading your list, get going and start your daily intentional practice.

PUSHING THROUGH

Other practical tools for pushing through those tough days and moments when you don't want to get going include creating a reward for yourself for that day. For example, I didn't want to write today. I got out of my usual habit of writing first thing in the morning and let the day get away from me. I was happy that I'd cleaned the house and run a few errands, but my daily goal of writing was still in front of me. To get myself going, I told myself I would get a treat when I got my writing done.

Notice that I said "when," not "if." That's an important distinction; don't make completing your commitment to yourself an "if" that you wonder about. As if it's a question whether or not it's going to happen. Tell yourself it is simply a matter of *when* it happens in your day.

You made this goal, and now you're going to meet it. When. Every day, it's just a matter of when and how you will incorporate it into your schedule.

Lastly, don't procrastinate. If you know you want to do it and it needs to be done, *do it*. Right now. Seriously. I know all too well how easy it is to tell yourself you will do something *after* you get organized—*after* you do something else, or when you have two minutes. Well, you have that time now, right now. Like the folks at Nike say, just do it. That way you can mark it off and be done with it. The time you spend doing your practice will be less than the time you spend stressing about it and then beating yourself up afterwards if you don't get it done. Ask yourself how you want to spend your energy: procrastinating doing the thing you wanted to do, or feeling proud that you kept your commitment to yourself?

This shouldn't be a chore. Remember, this isn't something you *have* to do. Your daily practice is something you've *chosen* to do, and probably for good reasons. It should be a treat or a gift you give yourself each day. This is something you get to do because you've made arrangements to make it happen—you've made the time and the commitment to yourself—so it should be something that you look forward to, not something you just muscle your way through. Don't check the box, own the box.

I'm going to ask you to stop for a moment and

think about the daily intentional practice you're contemplating. Have you written it down yet? If not, stop for a second and write it down. Have you practiced today? If you haven't, why not? What are the reasons you've chosen this particular thing for your daily practice? Stop reading and review the reasons you wrote down again. Now, what's your mantra? Can you repeat it to yourself now?

Own the box, don't check the box. Go practice now so you can pat yourself on the back sooner than later. You deserve it.

6.
Switch It Up

THE NEXT YEAR, 2014, WAS WHEN THINGS STARTED TO REALLY COME TOGETHER FOR ME. THAT WAS WHEN I REALIZED THIS DAILY PRACTICE THING WASN'T A ONE-OFF—that it was something I definitely wanted to continue. I wanted to keep adding to my life and finding new ways to improve. Now that I had seen progress and experienced success, I knew it wasn't something I was ready to let go of.

My newfound ability to finish had spilled over into other areas of my life, too. Work goals and other things I wanted to complete no longer seemed impossible.

That's another one of the rarely talked about benefits of a successful practice: it gets you into the mindset of being someone that accomplishes things. Once you taste that winning feeling in one area of your life, you start to believe you can achieve in other areas as well.

This year, I decided, I wanted to focus on something that wasn't related to my physical being. I wanted to choose something that was going to help me become a better person overall.

BETTER, STRONGER, FASTER

What does that even mean, to "be a better person"? Better than the next human? Better than I was the year before, the day before? It's different for every individual. In my case, I was focused on being the best Saydeah I could possibly be. But again, what does that really mean? How do you know when you're being the best *you* you can possibly be?

For some, the answer might be, "When you're perfect"—but that's an unrealistic target. No one is perfect. Although if you think of "perfection" as a goal in name only, and you recognize that it will always be a moving target, that might work for you. Whatever your concept of "better" is, whatever that means for you, every day is a chance to live up to that vision. For me, being better meant focusing on new and better approaches to dealing with the stress and negativity of life.

NEGATIVE NELLY

I had never really thought of myself as a negative person in the past, but the woman I was dating as 2014 rolled around remarked that I often had negative comments and approached things in a negative way. She shared that it was everything from small comments about other people who were acting in unintentionally rude or clueless ways to griping and complaining about daily life annoyances. She didn't quite say I was a negative person, but it was clear that the stressors in my life had made my external presentation one of pessimism—and I wasn't even aware of it.

After she said this, I started to notice how true it was. It was simple things, like yelling at a driver that cut me off in traffic and my constant impatience with slow service. I really value common sense, so when someone does something I consider "stupid" I take it personally and often react negatively—and I don't hesitate to share my thoughts with others.

I was surprised how much it bothered me to be thought of as a negative person—but it did, especially since the person who viewed me that way was someone I cared deeply about. I wanted to change that, and in more ways than one. First, I wanted to change people's perception of me as a negative person. Second, I wanted to change the way I actually *felt*. I didn't want to become a Pollyanna, hippie-dippy-type person that only *acted* happy because it was what I wanted the world to see; I actually wanted to *be* happy, truly and sincerely.

One of the many suggestions I discovered when I started researching the notion of happiness was to start by changing my perspective. One way to do this is to recognize all that you have by acknowledging what you are already grateful for. Gratitude can be an amazing cure-all when it comes to changing perspective.

OPPRESSION OLYMPICS

A note of caution here: when thinking about recognizing what you have and what you're grateful for, avoid getting into a game of the "Oppression Olympics."

What is the Oppression Olympics? According to Wikipedia, it is a "one-upmanship dynamic that can arise within debates about the ideological values of identity politics, intersectionality and social privilege. They have been described as verbal banter between marginalized groups who are trying to determine the weight of their many intersectionalities of oppression (race, gender, socioeconomic status, disability, etc.) to determine who has it the worst."

This jostling of who's worse off and who's got the greater burden can bleed into the idea of gratitude in really ugly ways that are beneficial to no one.

An example of Oppression Olympics is the debate that gay white men have it worse than straight black women—the argument being that homophobia is more difficult to deal with than racism, or is somehow a greater evil. Another example is women (universally) have a harder time getting ahead than those that grew up without a lot of material items or means—in other words, suggesting that sexism and misogyny are worse than classism.

As a gay, black woman who's definitely been poor at certain points of her life, I can tell you that all oppression is real and connected, and there are no hierarchies that matter. Every form of oppression is wrong; they all negatively affect our lives. One is not greater than another. So try not to participate in the Oppression Olympics. It's a game where everyone loses.

EVERYTHING IS RELATIVE

Another caution is that gratitude does not come from comparing yourself to others. The desire to compare yourself with others in negative or derogatory ways is a compulsion that should be avoided at all costs. For example, "Because I have a nice place to live, I should be grateful that I'm not a poor child in a developing country." Or, "Because I have two legs that function, I should be grateful that I'm not a paraplegic." This is not true gratitude.

Gratitude doesn't come from being "better off" than others. That kind of thinking is problematic for a number of reasons. First, you don't need to look to others to recognize what you have. Remember, it's not a game of who's got it worse. It's about simply appreciating what you have. Period. It's a steep hill when you get into that game, and once you get started, you'll slide down it quickly.

Second, if you actually talk to those "poor people"

you're comparing yourself to, you may find they are grateful for the circumstances they find themselves in. They are grateful because they've already figured out what's important in life, and it's usually not the things we're focused on. Yes, most would like the benefits of Western culture, like easy access to clean, running water and enough money to provide for their families, but they also appreciate what they have. Often those in the worst circumstances are the first to recognize that while they may be subsisting on mere dollars a day, in circumstances that most Westerners would find impossible, they have family, and friends, and a strong sense of community and faith. Their gratitude comes from some of the same things that my gratitude comes from: recognizing what you have, not focusing on what you don't. It's not looking at the glass and deciding that it is half full or half empty; it's looking at the glass and saying, "Look, I have a glass. And there's something in it." That's gratitude.

GRATITUDE PRACTICE

My gratitude practice for 2014, then, was to write down at least one thing that I was grateful for each day—the thought being that if you can acknowledge at least one thing that is positive in your life every day, that will slowly start to shift your perception about your overall life and maybe turn a Negative Nelly into a Positive Polly.

What would happen if you wrote down one thing you're grateful for every day? Do you think it would change the way you see your life? Could you come up with one new thing every day?

When I started the year, I did not think this would be a difficult task, and was actually kind of looking forward to it in a way that I hadn't looked forward to my daily intentional practices in previous years. But I soon discovered, to my surprise, that it was actually a little more difficult than I had anticipated.

The days when work was good, or I got see friends, and everything was going well, it was extremely easy to find something to be grateful for and write it down. But on those days when traffic was bad, and it took me over an hour to get to the office, and then I had a couple rough meetings, and then a friend bailed on lunch— those were the days when it was really hard to find something positive to acknowledge. And when you put a few of those bad days together, the challenge to be grateful became even harder.

That was when I discovered the key to a gratitude practice.

LOOKING FOR THE GRATITUDE

It turns out that gratitude practice is not about what you actually write down, it's about the act of trying to find something to document. As simple as it sounds, the process of *looking* for things to be grateful for is sometimes the thing that actually makes you grateful and changes your perspective.

If your house burned down and you lost everything you owned, could you write down one thing that you're grateful for? A gratitude mindset would say that if you have a pen and a piece of paper, that's a start. Then maybe it's about recognizing that you're alive and still drawing breath, and that's something else to be grateful for. How about the fact that firefighters got there in time to save you and your family? Perhaps you also have friends, family, and a community that can help you rebuild and get the supplies you need.

Again, it's not about comparing yourself to other people and being grateful that things aren't as bad for you as they are for others, but it is about acknowledging all the things *you* have, in whatever circumstances you have them. When you do have those crappy days where nothing seems to go right, those are the exact moments to stop and ask yourself what you're grateful for, and then acknowledge and appreciate the answer.

I realized throughout that year that there is always something to be grateful for, no matter what. Sometimes you might have to look a little bit longer and harder, but it's there. And again, it's not about being a Pollyanna or always trying to turn a frown into a smile. It is about small, subtle changes in your perspective that allow you to reframe any circumstance into something new, and hopefully even positive.

The other big lesson I learned through my gratitude practice is that once you're able to change your perspective in difficult circumstances, you will be able to change your perspective in life in general.

I was in a relatively new relationship in 2014, and I spent most of that year in new-relationship bliss, so a lot of my gratitude revolved around love and that relationship. Still, I recognized that when things weren't going well—when we'd had a disagreement or a bad day—I couldn't just rely on being grateful for her or our relationship. In order to maximize the benefits of my practice, I needed to push myself to move beyond the things I could easily see.

The process of purposefully and intentionally looking for something to be grateful for helped me to find things I never would have had in my life otherwise. When I pushed beyond the easy things and went deeper, I learned that a new perspective can be found anywhere, at any time, as long as you diversify your thinking.

I know I sound like a broken record, but this is where mindfulness, awareness, and intentionality come back in again. In order to push yourself beyond the easy, you have to be present and intentional in doing it. In order to move from just being grateful for my relationship and love to other areas, I needed to be intentional about *looking* for things to be grateful for each and every day. And by doing this—by actively pushing myself to explore other areas in my life to be grateful for—I learned the third lesson of a daily intentional practice: diversify your daily practice goals.

In looking at other things to be grateful for, I deepened my gratitude practice. I could see that the few minutes I had spent in the sun walking to meetings was something to be grateful for. Receiving a "just thinking of you and hope you're having a great day" text from a friend was another moment for gratitude, as was the fantastic lunch I had that day. By purposefully looking for moments of gratitude that already existed in my life, I was able to see how much I truly had.

Choosing something that was significantly different from the practices I'd chosen for my previous years pushed me in new ways I had not expected. I got benefits from this practice that I never anticipated— and by the end of 2014, I was a much happier and more positive person.

If you're still trying to figure out what your practice should be, think about starting with a gratitude practice. The benefits are amazing, and they can end up changing your life.

7.

Small Wins Equals Big Gains

EACH YEAR IN OCTOBER, WHEN I START THINKING ABOUT WHAT I WANT TO DO FOR MY DAILY INTENTIONAL PRACTICE THE NEXT YEAR, THERE ARE A COUPLE IDEAS THAT come to me that I immediately dismiss—often because they haven't resonated with me strongly when initially sitting down to think about it.

I've always felt like I'm a pretty intuitive person; I know when something *feels* right to me and when it doesn't. And when a new intentional practice doesn't feel right, I move on. But every once in a while, something that I've said no to in the past enters my consciousness again—and I've come to realize that if something comes back to me more than once, I shouldn't ignore it. I've learned that there is probably a reason it keeps coming up, and while I may not be ready for it the first or even the second time, I definitely shouldn't ignore it.

NO ESCAPING IT

Throughout 2014, the year of my gratitude practice, a number of people suggested that I start a meditation practice as a way to deal with the stresses of work and life. I had thought about meditation several times in the past, but had ignored it each time because I didn't think I was "that" person; on the contrary, I was the person that made fun of people that meditated. Literally. I used to make fun of my friends when they talked about going to silent meditation retreats. I was grounded and real and serious. I didn't do hippie-dippy, ethereal type stuff like that. *I am all about realism*, I thought. *I mean, I'm an INTJ damn it!*

I wasn't aware enough to know about the true history of meditation, so my idea of it was dirty hippies (why are they always dirty and why am I always picking on hippies?) that sat around moaning or humming mindlessly—or, even worse, a three-day silent meditation retreat where people gave you the evil eye for coughing. Both of those scenarios sound like my version of hell.

The other thing that really terrified me, when I thought about meditation, was the prospect of trying to quiet the many voices in my head. It feels like I'm always planning, thinking, or ruminating on something; the thoughts in my head never stop running around. And meditation seemed like it would require silence—complete and utter silence—in my head, which scared the crap out of me. I honestly didn't think I was capable of meditating, much less enjoying it, because of that silence.

More and more people I trusted and loved kept suggesting I look into meditation, however, and finally I knew it was something I shouldn't dismiss again. I didn't know where or how to start, but I knew that there was a reason it kept coming back to me. I decided I had to explore it further.

JUMPING IN VS. PREPARATION

Although I decided to make meditation my intentional practice for the next year by the end of October 2014, this was one of those times I did very little prep work before the year started. I think I figured that once I started meditating, I would just focus on quieting my mind and being silent.

That was my first big mistake. I should have done more research to learn more about the history and practice of meditation. I also should have spent more time thinking about and trying to determine what I wanted to get out of it. But because I was so scared of that year's daily intentional practice, I avoided thinking about it for as long as possible, and went into the year thinking I could wing it.

I was very wrong.

Part of being intentional in your practice is the work and preparation that goes on before you even start each day. When you practice swimming, you can't just jump in; you need to make sure you have your suit on and your cap and goggles ready first. Before you start basketball practice, you make sure you have your shoes on, laces tied, and a ball with air in it. It's really hard to do lay-up drills without a working ball.

Well, it's the same thing with your daily intentional practice. Do you have the right gear? Have you prepared correctly for your practice session? As you think about what you want to practice, be sure to think about what you'll need in order to be ready. Whether it's a physical item, like a book or shoes, or something less tangible, like access to time or a particular person, preparation is one of the keys to success for a building a consistent daily practice.

While I wasn't adequately prepared, I did manage to do one smart thing with my meditation practice: I started with a small and accessible goal that felt challenging but not impossible. My goal for the year was two minutes of meditation each day. That seemed like a real enough challenge, given where I was at the moment, but not completely overwhelming. For someone like me, who constantly has thoughts (and often worries) running through their mind, the idea of shutting everything down, even for only two minutes, seemed impossible at first. And frankly, it still does.

As modest as my goal was, January of that year was really hard. It was challenging for a number of reasons, including difficulties with my relationship, but mainly because I just couldn't quiet my thoughts. Every night for the first few days I sat down, set my phone timer for two minutes, and tried to clear my mind—but it quickly became clear that there was no clearing my mind.

Once I understood that making the thoughts quiet wasn't going happen through grit and sheer force of will, I focused on trying to repeat mantras during those two minutes (like my mantra for the year, or whatever "lesson" I thought I needed to work on). Sometimes I would repeat a reminder of what I wanted to try to accomplish the next day.

I found that mantras were definitely easier than silence, but even with their help, meditation wasn't easy—and it definitely wasn't enjoyable. Two minutes of repeating the same three words over and over got pretty stale pretty quickly.

Then, by happenstance—or the forces of the universe providing what you need, when you need it, depending on what you believe—I learned about a meditation app called Headspace. That's when everything changed for me.

PRACTICE GEAR

Headspace is a guided meditation app created by Andy Puddicombe, a former Buddhist monk with a degree in Circus Arts from De Montfort University in the United Kingdom. In 1994, Puddicombe stopped his studies to travel to Asia and train as a Buddhist monk as a way of coping with grief. His meditation training took him all over the world, to countries including Nepal, India, Burma, Thailand, Australia, and Russia, and eventually he landed at a Tibetan monastery, where he studied meditation with the monks. After that, he taught meditation in Russia for over four years before returning to the United Kingdom in 2004, where he took all that he'd learned over the years and partnered with Rich Pierson to create the app Headspace, which they launched in 2012.

As fate would have it, I was struggling with my daily mediation practice in February 2015 when Headspace was shared with me, and I was more than willing to give it a shot. While I liked the concept, however, I couldn't get past the timbre of Puddicombe's voice or his British accent, both of which I found distracting, and I didn't like the structure of having to go through Headspace's fixed introductory process to start. While I was becoming more and more convinced that an app was a good idea, it also seemed pretty clear that Headspace probably wasn't the right one for me. After sticking with it for a few days, I decided to check out other options that might be a better fit for me and my developing meditation practice.

As you progress with your daily intentional practice, don't be afraid to change things as necessary. One of the important elements of creating a new habit through practice is knowing when and how to tweak things. Knowing how to adjust and not just quit is how you get better. And finding the right tools to help make those adjustments is just as important. Recognizing that Headspace wasn't right for me could have been the end of it; I could have gone back to struggling with how to sustain a meditation practice on my own and sitting in painful silence. Instead, I continued to push forward and look for different alternatives, and I discovered a number of other options.

It was through this discovery process that I learned about Calm, an app founded in 2012 by Michael Acton Smith and Alex Tew Michael, a serial entrepreneur who had previously founded the kid's entertainment company Mind Candy and Moshi Monsters. Together, they developed Calm to bring meditation to the world, with a very similar mission to the Headspace team.

BREAKTHROUGH

Among the Calm app's many offerings is a selection of more than thirty meditation topics to choose from, including positivity, gratitude, forgiveness, creativity, calming anxiety, and compassion. When I initially started using the app I picked topics at random, usually based on how I felt in the moment. I sampled a number of them over the first few months I used the app (I'm not ashamed to admit that I used the "Emergency Calm" session more than once that year), and also checked out their seven-day introduction and other structured multi-day meditations—but similar to my experience with Headspace, the structured programs didn't work as well for me as the others.

At first, I stayed with my two-minute daily goal. As I sampled different categories, I slowly started increasing the time, and eventually got up to practicing ten minutes a day. When the "Daily Calm" feature—a unique daily meditation that addresses a new topic each day—was introduced, I immediately started using it. Daily Calm ties mindfulness concepts into the calendar in a topical and timely way—the topics often touch on real-world events, like Women's Day, Earth Day, or the first day of spring—and it worked for me in a way nothing else had.

I have continued to use Calm every day since I discovered their Daily Calm feature. My current streak is over 800 days of meditation without a break; some days I even meditate two or three times.

I'm not trying to sell you this app and I promise I don't work for them, but I can honestly say that I love the Calm app! It simply has changed my life. After using it for almost three years (as of this writing), I can tell you that I see the positive impact of meditation in my life every single day. Yes, I still get distracted when I sit to meditate, but the difference is, I'm aware of it now. That's the whole point of meditation: to increase your awareness of what's happening in the moment.

Because if you can get clear on what's happening in the moment, maybe you can recognize what you're doing in that moment; and if you know what you're doing, you can better understand *why* you're doing it. Start with the why, and you can change the what.

SHIFT YOUR PERSPECTIVE

Spoiler alert: meditation is just mindfulness. Actually, it's practicing mindfulness. There goes that practice thing popping back up again. Being mindful (or intentional) about everything we do is one of the keys to a happy and fulfilling life. You've probably figured that out already, given how many times I've said it in relationship to each year of my daily practice—but awareness really is the key. Just like changing a habit (or your life) starts with being intentional, meditation is a way to practice mindfulness, which is necessary to really get to the center of so many things in life. Once there's awareness, you're at least half of the way to making change happen. You can take that awareness and with it begin to change how you react to the circumstances you find yourself in. The change is in your reaction, not in the situation itself.

Meditation isn't going to change your circumstances in life. If you hated your job before, you will still likely hate it. If you had problems in your relationship before, those problems won't magically go away. The difference is, meditation will help you change how you *react* to those circumstances. Your awareness and thoughtfulness in each moment will help you shift your perspective, and hopefully your response, to the same situations as before. If that sounds familiar, it's because it's similar to the gratitude practice. Your circumstances don't change; your awareness of and perspective on them do.

While I initially started using Calm at night, in 2016 I switched to meditating in the morning because I wanted to incorporate a new daily intentional practice into my day. I found that starting my day with my meditation practice was even better than finishing my day with it. Now, at several points in the day, I ask myself what my daily meditation was that morning, and I repeat the key takeaway throughout the day, not only to make sure I'm hearing the lesson but to be thoughtful and intentional about the message and ensure I'm incorporating it into my life.

My daily meditation is now one of my favorite habits or rituals. For some, their first cup of coffee or breakfast is their favorite part of the morning. For me, it's the soft tones of the Calm app talking me through the Daily Calm topic of the day. No pun intended, but it calms me and helps me set an intention for what I want the day to be. What initially started as something I was scared to try has become a happy gift I can't wait to give myself each day. I truly enjoy it now— and when I don't get to start my day with it, I feel like something is wrong. There have probably been one or two days in the past two years when I didn't do my daily meditation right away after I woke up, and when that happened, I ended up feeling physically and emotionally off throughout the day—to the point that I stopped whatever I was doing later on to meditate immediately. Now I know that setting my alarm just ten minutes earlier to get that time for myself is absolutely worth it each and every day.

FIND YOUR OWN WAY

Of course, while I love the Calm app, technology isn't for everyone. I've talked to a few purists that hate the idea that my meditation practice is tied to my phone or any other form of technology. Meditation in its truest form is just you, but some people like to use a mat when they practice. Others have a special pillow they sit on. Some practitioners sit in a specific place or face a particular direction. Whatever works for you to help you focus in on awareness in the moment is what you should do.

I don't think I would have been as successful in my practice that year without the Calm app, and I know for certain I wouldn't still be meditating if I had kept stumbling through it on my own. I ran into a former coworker at an event recently, and as we were catching up he talked about how he'd started meditating with the Headspace app. It was so freeing and reinforcing to hear someone else talk about their meditation practice with the same joy and reverence I talk about my practice with Calm.

If you're interested in starting a meditation practice—or any practice, for that matter—do some advance preparation, experiment a little, and find the tools that work best for you. Don't worry about what other people think; just focus on finding the right fit for you.

The starting-small strategy works with more than just meditation. Whatever you're interested in for your daily intentional practice, think about starting small and growing from there. Build on your previous success, find the right tools, and continue to improve your practice every day.

8.

It's All About Love

AS A KID I WAS A VORACIOUS READER; I READ ALL THE TIME. AND WHEN I SAY ALL THE TIME, I MEAN ALL. THE. TIME. MY BROTHER AND SISTER WOULD OFTEN MAKE FUN OF me for having multiple books with me whenever we left the house. There was the book I was reading, the book I wanted to read next, and a third book, just in case I finished the other two while we were still out. Characters in books felt more like friends than the real-life kids I knew. And when I read I dreamed of doing the things the characters did.

In particular, I loved The Great Brain books by Brian Fitzgerald. If you haven't read them, you've missed out on great storytelling and lots of fun. I highly recommend checking them out. Those books took me to another world—a place where I wasn't the boring, quiet nerd but the cool, smart, and daring kid that led my friends into all sorts of adventures. A kid just like Tom Fitzgerald (aka "the Great Brain"), who, when things were at their worst and it looked like we were done for, could come up with some amazing and inventive way to get everyone out of the jam.

Reading introduced me to wild characters like Tom Fitzgerald and gave me windows and doors into other worlds and different people's stories. But as an adult, after working in the entertainment industry for a number of years and reading thousands of television and film scripts, I lost the ability to read.

No, I don't mean that I suddenly became illiterate and couldn't actually read anymore; I mean I lost my joy for the art of reading for pleasure. And with the loss of joy I lost the desire to sit down, carve out time, and actually do it. Add to that my graduate school program, which required that I read several hundred pages of dense academic theory each week, and I definitely wasn't a reader anymore.

As much as the joy of reading was gone for me, I wasn't ready to just let it go. I often lamented the fact that I wasn't reading anymore as it was something I really used to I love. And I knew that I would enjoy it again…if I could only find a way to do it.

IT'S ABOUT TIME

This is when I stumbled upon a very important lesson—two of them, in fact—that changed the way I thought about a lot of things in my life. They both relate to one phrase: *It's about time.*

This phrase has a couple different meanings. First, it refers to actual, measurable time—the literal minutes and seconds we have in our day. Second, it can mean "it's about time"—as in, it is past time to do it already. Like when a friend is late to meet you, you might say, "It's about time you got here."

Ask yourself, how much time do you have? Are you using it now (already) or later? *How* are you using it?

DO WHAT YOU LOVE

The other key lesson I learned is that it helps if you do something you love. I don't remember how or when the Holstee Manifesto was shared with me, but it hit me like a ton of bricks when I first read it.

Holstee is a company that offers guides, content, tools, inspiration, and an online community to help people live a more meaningful life. When brothers Dave and Mike Radparvar quit their jobs in 2009 to start a T-shirt project with their friend and cofounder Fabian Pfortmuller, they thought about building a company that would allow them "to live their dream while also making a lasting positive impact on the world." They sat down together and reflected on why they were doing it, and went on to create what has become known as the Holstee Manifesto, a set of guiding principles for themselves and the organization as it continued to grow.

Here is the Holstee Manifesto in full:

This is your life. Do what you love and do it often. If you don't like something, change it. If you don't like your job, quit. If you don't have enough time, stop watching TV. If you are looking for the love of your life, stop; they will be waiting for you when you start doing the thing you love. Stop over analyzing, all emotions are beautiful. Life is simple. When you eat, appreciate every last bite. Open your mind, arms, and heart to new things and new people, we are united in our differences. Ask the next person you see what their passion is, and share your inspiring dream with them. Travel often; getting lost will help you find yourself. Some opportunities only come once, seize them. Life is about the people you meet, and things you create with them so go out and start creating. Life is short. Live your dream and share your passion.

When I first read this, I had to stop and reread it a few times to really understand everything it was saying to me. Let's take a look at the manifesto line by line, starting with, "This is your life." How often do you really stop and think about that? Are you living the life you want to be living? I know there were many years when I didn't even think about the question because I was just muddling through. And when I did get around to asking the question, I certainly didn't have much of an answer to it. Now, after several years of consciously thinking about how I spend my time each day and what daily gifts I give myself, I can honestly, say, YES, this is my life and I'm living it the way I want to be living it.

The next line in the manifesto talks about doing what you love and doing it often. That was such an important discovery for me as I thought about returning to reading. I knew I loved reading and I knew I missed it, but I didn't think there was any way to add it to my already busy life. I mean, my job is not a forty-hour-a-week job, even in the lightest of times. And then there was my fitness and the time I needed to work out or go the gym. And although it was only ten minutes in my day, I had started meditating and knew I loved it and didn't want to give up that time either. How could I possibly add in something else?

I went back and re-read the Holstee Manifesto, and lo and behold, the answer was right there staring straight at me: "If you don't have enough time, stop watching TV."

PRIORITIES

For someone who once worked in the television industry and who truly *loves* television, this sounded preposterous to me. Stop watching TV? That was like asking me to stop eating sugar, or stop breathing. Both of which I clearly needed to live. What kind of non-fun-loving person would think that was an appropriate suggestion, much less the right solution? No way could that be the answer, right?

What I eventually realized was that I didn't need to stop watching TV altogether; I just needed to start being more conscious about what I was watching. Yep, there it is again—awareness and intentionality. It's it amazing how mindfulness ends up being the key to each and every practice, regardless of the specific goal.

So, consciousness about watching television; what does that actually mean?

In my case, it meant I needed to stop watching the stuff I wasn't really engaged with and be more aware of what I was doing, when I was doing it. If what I loved about TV and reading was enjoying great stories, then why did I find myself spending so much time watching reality shows with people I didn't care about doing ridiculous things in storylines that weren't engaging? That was time I could spend reading beautiful stories about characters I loved. So that's exactly what I did. I stopped watching TV aimlessly and without knowing what I was doing. Like my father used to say, I stopped letting the TV watch me, and I finally took control of the remote.

By eliminating shows I actually didn't enjoy and turning off the television for twenty to thirty minutes a night, I was able to start reading for pleasure again.

The Holstee Manifesto helped me to refine not only what I was doing but why I was doing it. If I wanted to do something I loved, like reading, I needed to find the time, and the time was there if I was more thoughtful about my TV watching. I found that not only was it possible to reduce it slightly, it was actually pretty easy. By the time the middle of the year came around, I was eagerly looking forward to that moment when the TV went off and I got to open a book. For the first time in a long time, it was a treat to jump into amazing stories and meet new characters again.

BITE BY BITE

My daily intentional practice for that year, 2016, was to read at least ten pages a day. When I started, ten pages seemed like an awful lot; I was someone who hadn't finished a book in several years, after all. Why did I select ten? Honestly, I don't know. I think I thought since ten works well in workouts (ten push-ups, ten sit-ups), ten pages a day seemed like a reasonable number. I often do things in sets of ten, so why not apply that to reading? Ten seemed doable, too; in the overall scheme of things, it wasn't a lot. In other words, I was utilizing some of the lessons I'd learned in previous years, including starting small and building from there, and embracing something that scared me a little and focusing on something I loved.

I also thought ten pages would make it easy to

remember where I was and track my reading from day to day, so I would know when I'd finished my reading for the day. (Yes, I believe in easy math.) And lastly, I reasoned that by reading ten pages a day, I could finish a 300-page book each month, enabling me to complete at least twelve books in the year.

When I sat down and thought about the idea of reading twelve books in one year, I was both scared and impressed by the enormity of the task—and knew I would get that dopamine release/sugar/ runner's high feeling if I was able to accomplish it. The reward feeling would be there each and every day that I read my ten pages; I would get to experience a sense of pride and accomplishment at the end of each month when I completed a new book; and at the end of the year, I could look at the twelve books I had read and bask in the success of my intention and completed goal.

I was lucky enough to get a gift of books from my partner in December 2015, so I was prepared with several books ready to go when the year started. I didn't have a plan, other than to try to pick books I thought I would enjoy and then read them. I didn't think I needed to prepare for the year, in the same way that I hadn't prepared for meditation, but I at least took the time to think about it. By being more conscious about how much time I spent watching TV—and, more important, about *what* I watched on TV—I was able to read at least ten pages each day that year. And by the end of the year, I hadn't read twelve books; I'd read *twenty-four*. Yes, twenty-four books! That's what happens when you do something you love, set an intention, and give yourself the tools and space to follow through on it.

How did I get through *twice* the number of books I thought I would in the year? By often reading more than ten pages a day. (And by the way, some of these were long books—over 500 pages—and only a couple of them were under 200 pages.) I read both fiction and nonfiction works, some of which I loved and couldn't wait to get to read each day, while others I enjoyed less and really needed to push myself to finish. I read books written by my talented friends Kamy Wicoff (*Wishful Thinking*) and Anondra "Kat" Williams (*Pat Greene*). I Columbused (when you "discover" something that is already there) Brené Brown and her fantastic work. If you haven't read *Daring Greatly* or *Rising Strong*, run out now and get them both. They will change your life. In addition, if you're looking for amazing stories of Africans in America (and elsewhere) definitely check out *Ghana Must Go*, by Teyae Salise, *Americanah*, by Chimimanda Adiche, and *Homegoing*, by Yaa Gyassi. All are beautifully written, engaging stories of Africans on and off the continent. And I discovered all of this on ten simple pages a day (plus a little extra).

THAT EXTRA EFFORT

As with every year and every practice I committed to, it was not always easy to get my reading in. Making it happen every day often necessitated some fore-thought and extra effort on my part. The extra effort came into play the moments when I was so tired I was barely keeping my eyes open, but I splashed water on my face, sat up, and kept reading. The forethought led me to take my book with me to the Warriors game so I could read it on the Bart train ride back home, or to take my book with me to work when I knew that I would be out late that night so I could get my reading done earlier in the day. Sometimes it meant skipping lunch with my colleagues to read a few pages because I had dinner plans that evening. Sometimes it required waking up a little earlier than usual because there wouldn't be time later in the day.

Whatever I needed to do, I did it, because that was the commitment I'd made to myself, and to the thing I loved. I also knew that I would enjoy reading once I got started, which made the extra effort more than worth it.

Are you going to be conscious about how you spend your precious moments each day? Are you going to put in the extra effort for the things you love? Remember, *it's about time.*

9.
What About Your Friends?

I'VE ALWAYS BEEN A PRETTY PRIVATE, RESERVED, AND SHY PERSON. AS A CHILD I WAS SO SHY IT WOULD HAVE BEEN MORE ACCURATE TO SAY I WAS AFRAID OF PEOPLE. I OFTEN hid behind my father's legs in social situations and people would remark how cute it was.

For me it wasn't cute; it was terrifying. Adults scared me. And other kids scared me even more. They were strange and unpredictable and often did things that made no sense to me.

At first, my shyness was made worse by the fact that my family moved every year. But as time went on, I started to learn that I could be a slightly different person at each new school, and each year I came out of my shell just a little bit. While I was still extremely shy, every new year was a little less painful than the year before it.

Ultimately, when we made our final move—to Fort

Worth, Texas—right before my sophomore year in high school, it got to the point that I actually had friends and was pushing myself to be outgoing. I even made myself step outside of my comfort zone and run for student council representative for my class—and to my surprise, I won.

That win started me on a path that eventually led to me running for and winning a spot on the Leadership Committee for the entire school. Family members from the East Coast couldn't believe that "little Saydeah" had actually done something so outgoing. The extremely shy kid they'd known years before, running for student office?

I share this story because it's important to know how very shy I am, and how private, when thinking about the fact that I actually wrote this book. I'm putting myself and my story out there in ways that are definitely not comfortable for me. I am an avowed introvert—someone who needs a lot of alone time to recharge and get energy. And like most introverts, I have a small group of really close friends that I love and treasure dearly. I am not the type of person who has or wants a large number of acquaintances and superficial connections. I don't like the idea of being "famous" and having strangers know me.

When I was a freshman in college, I participated in the Speaker's Bureau for the LGBT community. It meant going to dorms and other meeting groups on campus and talking about my coming out story and answering questions from other students. I was willing to do this because at the time I was the only out frosh (Stanford's word for first-year students), and I wanted to make things better for other first-year students. It was a little scary and intimidating at first, but after realizing that I was just telling my story, each session got easier.

The one thing I could never get used to though was people walking up to me on campus and recognizing me. They would say they'd heard me speak and were usually kind and complimentary, but I never got used to strangers knowing who I was. I know a lot of people out there dream of being famous, but I never have and never will. It's actually a pretty scary thought for me. I've often joked that I'm a misanthrope, but that isn't exactly true. I don't hate mankind. Somewhere deep down I actually do love people, even if I am usually disappointed by them.

Even today, I am still a little scared by people in general—not in the traditional sense of the word, but more from an awkwardness perspective. The wildly successful *Awkward Black Girl* web series created by Issa Rae (a fellow Stanford alum) is partly the story of my life. The main character is prone to finding herself in all sorts of uncomfortable situations involving a love triangle and her crazy best friends. I may not get myself into all the ridiculous predicaments she does, but we do share the same uncertainty around what to do in certain social settings.

There are folks who always know the right thing to say or do in a given situation, and then there are people like me. Like my father, I can be extremely charming in certain contexts; while it seems like it comes naturally, however, it is actually something I have to work at considerably. And it always takes a lot of energy out of me when I do. Remember, I'm an introvert. One of the great things about getting older is that while you may never get good at knowing how to interact, or be less awkward in certain situations, you at least stop caring about what other people think. Becoming less and less insecure about those things as I've gotten older has been such a blessing.

ONE SQUARE INCH

Not stressing out about other people's opinions of you doesn't mean you never think about other people. I care about what my friends and the people who love me think; I just don't care what a random person on public transportation or a salesperson at a store thinks. In *Daring Greatly,* Brené Brown talks about the fine line between caring so much about other people's opinions that we lose ourselves and risking not caring at all and losing our ability to connect with others. She encourages us to take a one-inch-by-one-inch square piece of paper and write down the list of people whose opinions matter to you. That list should consist only of people who love you not in spite of your imperfections but because of them. She goes on to say that if you need more room on your paper, you need to keep editing the list.

One inch by one inch is not a lot of real estate, so use that space wisely. Don't waste it on people whose opinions shouldn't count when it comes to how you view yourself. Remember the "Life Changing Magic of Not Giving a F*ck"? The people who are worth spending your time, money and energy on should be on the list. No one else.

Whose opinions do you really trust and value because they're coming from the right place? Who is more concerned with helping you grow than tearing you down? When faced with difficult decisions or moments when you're questioning yourself, come back to your square-inch piece of paper and talk to the people whose names are on that list. That same group is also the team you can turn to for another important step in your daily intentional practice: sharing your daily practice with friends and loved ones.

LET YOUR COMMUNITY SUPPORT YOU

This is such a simple and brilliant strategy, I'm embarrassed to admit it took me a few years to both understand and embrace it.

At first, I was reticent to tell anyone about what I was doing because of my general shyness. But over time I realized I wasn't sharing because it became something

I was embarrassed by—and for no real reason. Aside from a few friends volunteering vegetable suggestions in the early years, I wasn't very open about my daily intentional practice.

Gradually, when I found myself explaining more often why I was choosing to leave a party early because I wanted to get up and work out, or had brought a book with me to an event because I wanted to be prepared to carve out time to read later, it became easier to tell people what I was doing. And that's when I learned the second benefit of talking to friends: most people actually want to support you. When I started sharing my daily intention with friends, the amount of encouragement I received from them was amazing and uplifting and far surpassed anything I would have thought possible.

Eventually, I realized that part of the reason I hadn't been saying anything about my daily practice before was because I was scared that if I failed, people would see me as a failure. And I know a lot of people that struggle with this particular fear—of not only failing and disappointing themselves but failing and disappointing *others*, especially those that have supported them over time.

But what I've found is that the opposite is true: People are often impressed that you're even starting something like this. They want you to succeed, and they recognize that the endeavor you're undertaking is a big one. There's an old sports adage that you miss every shot you don't take, so you have to step up to the starting line and at least try if you want to be in the game. Very badly mixed metaphors aside, the point is, people are often much more supportive than you think they will be—and if you give them a chance, you will likely be surprised.

SHARING IS CARING

The other lesson I learned by sharing my daily intentional practice is that people often get inspired and want to join in themselves. I can't tell you how many people I've met over the past six years who have been inspired to start their own daily growth projects after learning about mine—and who have changed their lives because of it. I've had strangers tell me that they've started their own practice after I've shared my story with them.

That feeling—knowing that I've impacted someone else in a positive way, no matter how small—is amazing, and it helps give me the strength to keep pressing forward with my daily practice, especially on those days when it is particularly hard.

Sharing your story also gets other people invested in your success in a way that makes it personal and helps build connection and relationships. All of my friends know how much I dislike vegetables, so when eating them was my daily practice, having friends ask me which one I'd eaten that day helped us bond. They gave me suggestions of vegetables I hadn't tried before, new ways to prepare them—anything to help me achieve my goal. I was so appreciative of their support and love throughout the year that I got more comfortable sharing other initiatives with them, and ultimately just sharing more about my life in general. That's how you build connection with others.

As I mentioned before, my partner got me several books for Christmas the December before I started my daily reading practice. Receiving support like this from friends and family in preparation for your daily practice can make the difference between failure and success. Inviting people on the journey with you often leads to new journeys for them, and enhances yours. Some of my friends have even helped me come up with new practice ideas for the year to come. However your loved ones contribute, the connections you build with others when you're helping each other on the path to success are amazing and invaluable.

DO WHAT FEELS GOOD TO YOU

How you share your daily intentional practice doesn't matter as much as the fact that you're sharing. Putting yourself out there can be a little scary sometimes—at least I know it is for me—so feel free to be creative about how you share. I have friends who have taken to social media with a daily recap of what they did and how they practiced that day. There are even tools like reminder apps and websites that allow you (and others) to track your practice goals—like 750words.com, for instance, which helps user track their daily writing challenge. Even a simple blog (which you can set up relatively easily, and for free) can be another tool you use to share your daily intentional practice.

Sharing gives you an opportunity to be honest about any struggles you may be having and gives people an opportunity to support you. For example, a friend of mine shared her month of no sugar and was utterly vulnerable with everyone on those days, and in those moments, when she just had to have some sugar. With a quick tweet or Facebook post in moments of extreme struggle, she instantly had friends (and sometimes strangers) chiming in with encouragement and suggestions—"get some protein," "take a walk," "jump up and down for thirty seconds." It was a team effort to get her through that rough moment and help her do anything other than eat sugar in that moment. Again, people generally want to be helpful, so the challenge is really figuring out if you're going to be vulnerable enough to reach out to them and give them the opportunity to help.

Another way people share their daily practice is in person with a group or team. One of the many reasons I love Crossfit is the community aspect. In those times when I don't want to get through a workout (which doesn't happen that often), I have a crew that supports and encourages me and reminds me of the high I'll feel when I get it done. They know the struggle intimately so their advice and encouragement is real and valuable. Sometimes they're even more proud of me than I am of myself when I reach a new PR (personal record) or push through a really difficult workout. That's the joy behind having group support.

Another friend of mine who was tackling a new challenge each month created a really creative infographic to track her success, and she shared it in all of her social media profiles (Facebook, Twitter, Instagram, and Snapchat). It got to the point where people were waiting for and expecting a new infographic every week; they would even proactively ask about it if she was a little late to post a new update. That's the beauty of sharing: creating excitement in others and inviting them into your success.

Another way to share is to create an online calendar, or to put up a physical one somewhere where others can see it. Every time you practice and do what you say you're going to do, you put a big "X" on your calendar. That's it. You may be surprised at how well it actually works. Science tells us that once we see a row of X's on our calendar, we feel motivated not to break the chain. So that means we get up and practice again, we do our task again and again, and every time we check off another box we get that satisfying feeling that we accomplished something.

Remember, when you're trying to build up a new

habit, it doesn't matter how well you do it at first; what's important is the fact that you've done it at all. That's the point of practice: to get better with repeated efforts. If you think of it this way, the "how well" will come naturally—you'll start to get better and better and excel over time, you just have to keep going back out there and trying. And best of all, when the end result does come and you're performing well, it's not the light at the end of the tunnel, it's just an added bonus. Because it really is about the journey, not the destination.

DO AS I SAY, NOT AS I DO

I'll be honest: I haven't been great about using the advice about sharing myself. I'm still really shy and pretty nervous about sharing my daily practice. But it's one of things that I'm pushing myself to do more and more these days, even though it scares me. While I've been sharing my intentional practice with close friends for a few years now, I've also started telling people I don't know well, sometimes even relative strangers, about what I'm doing. I'm still often surprised, though by now I shouldn't be, by how supportive people are, even people I don't know well.

Which leads me back to why I'm writing this book again. It's because, like I said at the beginning of all this, I want to help others—to share what I've learned with other people. To help support others. Finally, I'm taking this lesson to heart. Sharing is caring, so

I'll share something else. I've decided that my daily intentional practice for 2018 will be to perform one small act of kindness each day. It can be something as small as letting someone go in front of me in traffic, or buying a cup of coffee for a stranger, or helping out a sick friend.

The idea is to intentionally and purposefully look for moments throughout the day where I can be kind to someone one. I've also decided I'm going to share my daily act of kindness with the world publicly each day. My hope is that each small act of kindness on my part will inspire others to perform their own small act of kindness, creating a tidal wave of kind acts. I've chosen this practice now because as I was reflecting on the past seven years, I realized that all of my daily practices have focused on me—on making myself a better person. Now, I believe, is the time to look externally and see if I can be a small part of making the world a better place. I hope you'll join me.

10.

Not Easy, Gets Easier

ONE OF THE BIGGEST LESSONS I'VE LEARNED THROUGHOUT THIS JOURNEY, AND ONE OF THE MOST IMPORTANT PIECES OF ADVICE I CAN GIVE YOU ABOUT STARTING A DAILY intentional practice, may sound somewhat confusing at first glance: this is not easy, but it does get easier.

No matter what you've chosen as your daily practice, and regardless of how long you plan to stick with it, this undertaking will not be easy. I know you probably want to hear that it will be easy to walk thirty minutes every day for a month, or read every day for six months, or work on your craft projects consistently for a year, but the brutal truth is that practicing is hard, and trying to create a daily intentional practice will be difficult. Period. If you're trying to make real change happen, it won't be easy. Change rarely is.

If it helps to know this, your daily practice also

probably won't be the hardest thing you've ever done. I'd like to think that designation is reserved for something truly important, like rearing children, watching a parent pass away, or fighting a serious illness. These things are, unfortunately, some of the hardest things you'll have to do in life. Your daily intentional practice won't rise to that level; it will, however, challenge you.

Why do I tell you this now? With so many people selling quick solutions for everything from losing weight to getting rich, and trying to tell us that technology makes everything easy, why on earth would I want to tell you something will be hard? Simple: I think it's important to know the truth before you start. Being aware of what you're getting into is part of being mindful and conscious of what you're doing. And if we've learned anything so far, it's that in order to make a daily practice work, you have to be intentional.

For my part, I like to know when something is hard from the beginning; that way, I can get myself ready. It helps me calibrate my mindset and prepare myself for what's ahead. As they reminded us repeatedly in *Game of Thrones*, "winter is coming," and it's time to prepare for it. While you don't need to prepare for White Walkers and other demons, you do need to prepare yourself for your practice if you're going to be successful. And part of preparing yourself mentally means recognizing this won't be easy, especially in the beginning.

EASE INTO IT

For pretty much every year of the past seven years that I've engaged in a daily intentional practice, January and February have been the toughest months for me. The struggle is real as I get used to a new practice and start figuring out how to make it a habit. During that time, I'm trying to gauge out how to work it into my life in a way that makes sense, and it takes time to do that. So know that starting out in January (or whenever you begin your practice), things will be hard. It is not an easy thing to get yourself to do something new, and no matter how much you *want* it, the actuality of *doing* it is often difficult.

I'm always curious about the divide between wanting something so badly that you can feel it in your bones and still being unwilling or unable to *do* the things you need to in order to get there. That is precisely what makes this practice so hard—and so rewarding, when you accomplish it. So many people can't get over the hurdle of merely talking about what they want to achieve in life; they spend all of their time and energy discussing it and never actually doing it. You know those people—the talkers that never stop talking. That's where you're different: you're going to *do* something about it. And you can start by recognizing that the *doing* part will not be easy.

As I mentioned before, over the course of the year I decided to eat one serving of vegetables a day, there were many nights in January and February when I had to get up from bed and eat a baggie of carrots or warm up some broccoli because I had forgotten to eat my vegetables earlier in the day. It was only after recognizing that it was such a pain in the butt to get up and eat my vegetables and brush my teeth a second time that I started thinking about ways to make it easier for myself. What I was doing wasn't sustainable; I couldn't keep it up for the rest of the year. So I came up with two ideas, the first of which was simple: I would write down the vegetable for the day in my calendar right after I ate it.

DOCUMENT YOUR SUCCESS

In addition to sharing your challenge and success with friends and family, tracking your success can be really helpful. After I started writing down my vegetable immediately after eating it, I was able to look at my day planner throughout the day—and definitely at least before I brushed my teeth—and know if I had eaten my vegetables for that day. Having a simple visual cue to remind myself of the day's practice took a little bit of the thinking out of it. And the minute that you can take the "thinking" out of anything, the closer you are to creating a habit and making your practice easier.

Since that year, I've continued to document my intentional practice every day, so I can see my daily success as it happens. As I track what I do during the day, I look to the bottom of my planner to see if I've completed my intentional practice for the day, and if I haven't, I figure out how and when I'm going to make it happen. Often, I do this the night before, when I'm thinking about what my schedule for the following day will look like. That's where preparation—and yes, you guessed it, awareness and intentionality—comes into play. The same mindfulness and intentionality we're seeking in a meditation practice transforms to the physical awareness of what we're doing as we write down and mark off our daily practice each day. We're trying to create a habit here—to add something new to our lives—and that means doing things differently.

MAKE ROOM FOR YOUR PRACTICE

The other idea I came up with to make my vegetable-eating practice easier on myself was to try and incorporate it into my lunch. By picking a meal I had every day, no matter what, I could ensure I got my practice done, and done well, before bedtime. At the time, I sometimes I only drank a protein shake for breakfast and often wouldn't eat dinner at all, but I ate lunch every day. It took me a couple months to get down to it and really figure that out, but once I did, I realized that incorporating my daily vegetable practice into lunch was the smart move—and it wasn't that difficult, either.

By March I was in the habit of having something with a vegetable at lunch and immediately writing it down.

By determining the best, and easiest, way to incorporate my daily vegetable consumption into my existing life, I was able to achieve the change I desired. There's a definite rhythm to the year, and before the start of the summer what had seemed impossible in January was becoming easier each and every day.

As you think about how you can make room in your life for your daily practice, keep in mind that it's sometimes about shifting an existing pattern and incorporating something new, and sometimes it's about creating a new schedule altogether. For me, structuring my daily routine around the completion of my goal came naturally, because I'm a routine person. I could probably eat the same thing every day for most of my life and feel okay about it. I wish we all had a basic work uniform, so I would never have to decide what I was going to wear. That's how much I like routine and not having to spend time thinking about and making those kinds of decisions. But what about people like my friend Angela, who can't stand the idea of a routine so much that she rarely wears the same thing twice? And what about those times when my routine has to change due to work or social commitments?

Well, whether you're anti-routine like Angela or forces outside your control disrupt your schedule, you have to think about things even more. You have to be even more thoughtful and intentional about how you're going to incorporate your intentional practice into your day. The year I was working out at least thirty minutes a day, for example, I had a business trip to France and an early flight out on my last day. A very early flight: I had to be at the airport by four thirty in the morning, and my hotel was at least thirty to forty minutes away. Which meant if I wanted to get a thirty-minute workout in, I would either need to wake up at three o'clock in the morning or figure out how to work out when I got home from a very long international flight (which you and I both know that wasn't going to happen).

Rather than start with a lie to myself—*Oh, I can and will do it later*—I honestly assessed the situation and realized that my only option was to get up and get in my workout before my flight. I'm a morning person, so generally speaking I would rather wake up early to get something done than stay up late. Even I recognized that setting my alarm for 3:00 a.m. in order to work out before a flight was slightly crazy—but that's what you do when you want to make change happen. You make different choices and structure your life in a way that will allow you to achieve your goal.

Making things easier for yourself throughout the year requires making them automatic to some extent. When you've created room in your life by making different choices and creating an easy structure to make your practice automatic, it truly becomes a habit—and that's when you don't have to put in as much effort and work into making it happen.

To go back to the example of brushing your teeth: you don't have to talk yourself into doing it every night, it's just part of your routine. And that's the goal for your daily practice—to make it part of your routine. Don't get me wrong, there's still work and intentional effort involved every time you set out to do something different from what you used to do, but the more automatic you make it, the less you'll struggle to get it done. When you can turn your brain off so much that you're executing your practice without thinking—when you're just doing it—you'll know you've created a habit.

EXPERIMENT

The more you keep up with your daily practice, the more you'll find that it has actually become a habit. Once you've incorporated it into your life, you'll feel like it has magically gotten easier.

Part of figuring out how to get to this point is knowing yourself and your life. For me, writing down my daily practice every day in my day planner has become a given. No matter what the pursuit, I write it down my calendar right after I've completed it every day. On the days when things seem especially hard and I feel like I just can't do it that day, I flip backwards through my planner and look at my previous successes. I remind myself of the times when things seemed especially hard and I pushed through anyway, and I use those moments to give me the encouragement and motivation I need to keep going and to recognize that I have the strength and capacity to practice again today. Even if today is a hard day. Especially if today is a hard day.

Knowing yourself also means knowing what works best for your schedule and your natural body rhythms. Like I said, I'm a morning person, so working out in the morning works well for me. My writing is better in the morning, too, because I generally have more energy then. You might prefer an afternoon run or an evening workout. Do that. Do you. Try different things, experiment, and figure out what's right for you.

As I mentioned in Chapter 7, the year I started meditating, I began by meditating at night, before I went to sleep. And that initially worked for me—but when I wanted to read the following year, I found that reading at night was best for me, so I switched to meditating in the morning. Wouldn't you know it—I actually got more out of meditation when I did it in the morning, and I enjoyed it more, too. That schedule worked better with my body rhythm.

As you can see, I had to experiment a bit to figure out what worked for me and what didn't. I encourage you to do that as well. Play with different times of the day as you begin your daily practice. Experiment with different ways of tracking your success each day, too. The more you do that, the more you'll realize that while this is hard, it does get easier as you incorporate your practice at those times and in those ways that make the most sense for you.

Each day you're practicing, you're getting closer to making your practice a habit. And that will eventually make things easier—I promise.

11.
Rewards

ONE THING I HAVE NOT BEEN GREAT ABOUT THROUGHOUT THE YEARS OF MY DAILY PRACTICE IS REWARDING MYSELF. AS WE LEARNED FROM DUHIGG, REWARDS ACTUALLY comprise one of the most important parts of this process, and I would encourage you to be smarter than I was.

I've always said some of us are carrot people and some of us like the stick. Meaning, some people are better motivated by rewards—e.g., the carrot—and the opportunity to get something positive for doing something well, while other ("stick") people are driven by the fear of being punished or getting in trouble for not achieving a goal.

While everyone can be moved in one direction or another by both approaches, I believe that we're all naturally inclined, or have been trained, toward one. This will probably come as no surprise to you at this point in my story, but I am a more of a stick person. Couple my self-discipline with the way I can be naturally hard on myself, and it's clear that while I am a people pleaser and want to make others happy, I am also deeply driven by the fear of punishment.

I was pretty much always a rule follower as a kid—which is not that remarkable, when you think about the fact that I was so shy and introverted. When you break the rules you draw attention to yourself, and that was always the last thing I wanted to do. In addition to naturally being inclined to follow the rules, I was also pretty fearful of the stick and the admonishment that came when I got into trouble.

Even now, as an adult, it's fair to say that about 70 percent of the things I do are driven by a desire to avoid getting in trouble. I don't jump the line; I pay my fare on the bus, even when no one is around to notice. I want to follow the rules. This is probably a good quality to have most of the time—especially as a Black person in America. When you look like me, you can get killed for not following the rules (and oftentimes even if you do, but that's another book).

Unfortunately, though my rule following may keep me safe, it also means I don't focus enough on the other side of things: the reward.

WHY THE CARROT MATTERS

Why are rewards so important? If we look back to the discussion of the habit loop, we can see that it's not a stick or punishment at the end of a cycle that causes a habit to be created or changed; it's a reward. Either changing your routine to get you to the reward or changing the reward after your routine, is the intrinsic virtuous reward cycle that we all go through. When we do something pleasurable and get that feeling, those endorphins, that high, we want to do it again.

I certainly get that feeling when I'm running. I often experience the "runner's high" that people talk about, which makes it easier to push through the hard moments, and also easier to get back out for the next run. In fact, it makes it so I *want* to go on a run, because I'm eager to get that feeling again. This is very similar to what happens with drug use (though hopefully without all the negative and often brutal consequences of drug addiction). In fact, when I was recently injured and couldn't run for two months, I actually went through feelings of withdrawal, and though it made no logical sense, I wanted to run so badly that I actually tried to a few times. Of course, I could barely move my knee and probably set my recovery back trying to, but that's how strongly I felt about wanting to run to get that rush of endorphins, my reward, and the pleasurable feeling I desperately craved.

While mental benefits can be pretty powerful, the

reward doesn't have to be something like the runner's high or the pride of having achieved your goal. It can also be tangible. I recommend that, somewhere in there, you sprinkle in a few tangible rewards that appeal to you. And remember, they need to be things that work for you. I love cupcakes and they would probably be my preferred reward, but if that's not the right one for you, find something that is.

RIGHT REWARDS

How do you figure out what the right reward for you might be? Close your eyes and think about what you would really enjoy. Is it a food or beverage? Is it a non-edible physical item, like new shoes, a new dress, or a new hat? Maybe it's an experience, like going to a concert or jumping out of a plane. Whatever works for you is what you should focus on. However—and this part is important—your reward should not take away from, or harm, your ultimate goal or your daily practice. It shouldn't take away from what you're trying to accomplish or set you farther back from what you're trying to add to your life. As long as it meets these criteria, then go for it.

Let's say your daily intentional practice is to walk a mile each day and get in better physical shape. If your reward is a fully loaded pizza each day, well, you're not doing yourself any favors; in fact, you're harming your overall goal and intention. You're essentially ruining your practice session every day with your reward. If your daily practice is to save $10 each day in order to go on vacation at the end of the year, then your weekly or monthly reward shouldn't be to blow that money on new clothes. And if you can make your reward something that's complementary to your overarching goals *and* something you want, then that's even better.

Rewards should be big enough that they matter to you and are motivational; at the same time, they should be small enough that they don't completely take over why you started your daily intentional practice in the first place. You can't be doing it just for the new blouse each week, or the new toy. You've got to keep in mind the true reason you want to add this aspect to your life.

This is another good time to stop and think about the reasons you identified in Chapter 3 for starting this journey of change. Go back and review what you wrote down. Do your reasons still resonate with you?

Now think about a few things you can give yourself as a reward that will complement your overall goals. How frequently you reward yourself is up to you, but remember not to let the carrot overtake why you're doing this in the first place. The journey and process of creating a new positive habit should also be a reward in and of itself.

REWARD YOURSELF IN INTERVALS

If you've chosen a yearlong practice, another important key is to reward yourself throughout the process
and not just at the end of the year. Whatever length of
time you've chosen to practice, find points within that
period when you can step back, assess, and hopefully
reward your progress. Small but meaningful rewards
throughout will help you stay on top of your goals in a
more consistent way.

Be aware that while you're developing a habit for the
thing you're trying to add to your life, you don't want to
also create a negative habit by *needing* a reward every
time you do something. Try and keep your practice
from becoming dependent on your reward. You don't
want to inadvertently create a new habit of needing an
extrinsic reward for your new routine.

Lastly, give yourself a big reward when you complete
your ultimate goal. At the beginning of your practice
process, think about what that ultimate reward for all
your hard work and sacrifices could look like. Pick
your reward now, and use it as part of your motivation
to get to your overall goals, knowing that every day
you practice gets you closer to that reward.

12.
Game Time

I'M A PUZZLE TYPE OF PERSON AND I GET EXCITED WHEN I GET TO PLAY GAMES. I LOVE SOLVING RIDDLES AND MYSTERIES AND CHALLENGES ALONG THOSE LINES. I CAN turn just about anything into a game—even random things you would never think of. For example, if I'm putting my laundry away, I make it into a game of how quickly I can fold my jeans. Is there a new way I can come up with that will make it faster? Can I beat my last record?

Yes, I know it's pretty geeky, but I love the idea of constantly getting better and doing better than I've been or done before. Note that I'm not super competitive with other people, so for me, it's not about being better than someone else; it's always about being better than *I* was before.

It's another thing I love about Crossfit; that it is

generally a battle against yourself and your last performance. When you brag, it's about beating *your* previous performance or a PR, not someone else's. We're all trying to be our very best selves, regardless of what other people are doing. Yes, there are competitions where you test yourself against others, namely the Crossfit Open and the Crossfit Games, but even then, when elite athletes are going head to head, they're mainly focused on their own performance, not on what their competitors are doing. Many aspects of the competition are about beating the time, not necessarily the man or woman next to you.

Even when individuals go head to head in Crossfit events, they understand that everyone has specific strengths and weaknesses that balance out the competition. For example, I find upper-body movements like pull-ups and pushups relatively easy compared to most women, because I have pretty strong arms. But my poor flexibility means I can't do front squats or other basic gymnastic movements that require good movement correctly. So my Crossfit friends celebrate when I learn a new movement just as much as I celebrate when they're able to do a push up or pull-up. It's all about being the best *you* you can be.

Taking that same idea of turning things into a game, one helpful approach I've used with my daily intentional practice is to have fun with it by turning it into a game as often as possible. I'll stop here for a second and say that if you're not someone that likes games and puzzles, this strategy might not be for you. Trying to turn your practice into something you intrinsically don't like is generally not a good strategy if you want to keep doing it. But if you like solving problems and riddles as much as I do, this is a good opportunity to put that skill to use.

GAME THEORY

How do you make a game of your daily practice? First, you need to begin by creating rules. Every game has its own rules and structure, and you'll have to come up with the ones that work for you and your challenge. It can involve the way in which you complete it, the time it takes you, or something else entirely; whatever you do, try to make it fun. Examples from some challenges I've given myself in my daily intentional practice include how many pages I can read in ten minutes and how many minutes I can add to my meditation practice each day. I try to make it fun and simple by finding ways to gamify it.

If you're not familiar with the idea of gamifying, it's one of the many hot trends that's taken over the tech industry in the past few years. The theory is that pretty much anything that can be tracked or measured can be improved, similar to a video game. Everything from the Lyft or Uber driver performance rating system to Netflix and Amazon's consumer-driven recommendations are examples of different versions of game theory in action.

Game theory in social situations examines how people interact with one another when trying to achieve their own individual goals. Specifically, decision theory focuses on the choices we make and analyzes why and how we make those decisions, what information we look at, and why we prioritize certain pieces of data over others. When Netflix recommends a new romantic comedy to you because you watched *Pretty Woman*, that's game theory and decision analysis, applied through their complex algorithm. They are using specific data points to make what they hope are relevant recommendations, all to make you buy more products on Amazon or stay engaged longer on Netflix.

Why should you try to apply game theory to your daily practice? Because research says that certain parts of the brain get activated when we play games—and those areas are similar to what we use when we create a new habit. Great video game players are good because they play games a lot. They spend a significant amount of time creating new mental patterns and reinforcing muscle memory to the point that they can anticipate certain aspects of the game in advance. The first time they play a new game is nothing compared to their performance after playing that game for hundreds of hours.

Playing video games might not be how you like to spend your days, but you can still cultivate a habit by creating new tunnels in your mind for the movements involved in your daily practice. That change further cements the habit you're trying to create.

This is part of the reason why playing video games constantly can become a negative habit and potentially be bad for you: because your brain actually becomes rewired when you do anything repeatedly. For example, if you constantly think of yourself as a loser or failure, you will start to believe it, and no matter what happens, that version of your story will remain true in your mind.

I know this because I used to spend a lot of time thinking really negative things about myself—so much so that I couldn't hear it when people I loved and trusted told me otherwise. Other examples of how we wire our brains for the things we don't want in life include more tangible habits like smoking and biting your fingernails.

If you can wire your brain for these negatives, of course, you can certainly use the same tactics to rewire your brain and add positive habits to your world. You can rewire yourself for the things you want in life just as easily you can rewire your brain to the things you *don't* want. They key is being conscious, aware, mindful, and—there it is again—*intentional* about what you're wiring into your brain.

Think about how you can apply some of this knowledge and these same tools to your daily intentional practice. We are what we do when we do it repeatedly, so think about what *you* can do repeatedly that will create a positive story about yourself.

GAME WINNINGS

The other important part of games is that you often get small and big rewards as you advance. In Monopoly you get money or properties on your way to dominating and winning the game. In Pac-Man you eat little pieces of fruit as you move from level to level. The same idea applies to gamification; you should make sure you're reaping small and big rewards as you advance through your "game." Perhaps, for example, you walk an extra half a mile one night, so you get have some of your favorite ice cream. (Just some, not the entire pint, okay?) Or you write an extra 1,000 words one day, so you get to re-watch that favorite movie of yours. Think back to the rewards you came up with in the last chapter and how you can apply some of the smaller and bigger ones throughout your daily practice.

Remember, the game itself is also a reward as you go through, so don't get overly focused on the other things you can win in the game. Apply the rewards throughout your practice as icing on the proverbial cake; don't make them the cake itself. And remember, a game should build over time. Take poker as an example: you don't just suddenly get all the chips or points; you accumulate them slowly, bit by bit. As you apply game theory to your daily intentional practice, adopt this same approach.

Lastly, your rewards don't always have to be something tangible. As always, the key is to make it fun, period. If you're not having fun at some point, you're not doing it right. Note that I said "at some point"; we already know this won't be easy and there will be parts of this process and certain days that will be particularly hard. But if you're not having some fun too, then why are you doing it? Just as you need to be able to remember the good times you've had together and the reason why you're still in the relationship when you and your partner are having a hard day, you also need to have positive memories involving your daily intentional practice when the going gets tough.

This is a good time to go back to the beginning. What are the reasons you wanted to start a daily intentional practice in the first place? Go back and look at your mantras and say them out loud. What do they remind you of? Do they still resonate with you? Can you use them now to think about how to turn your practice into a game?

Using your mantras, inventing new rewards, and making a fun game of your daily intentional practice are all tools that will help you through this journey. But what about those times and days when you really, truly can't? When you've woken up early, when you've restructured your life, when you have honestly done everything and anything you can, and for some reason—likely one beyond your control—you just can't complete the day's daily practice? What then?

13.

Compassion

WHAT THEN, INDEED? WHAT HAPPENS WHEN YOU CAN'T OR DON'T MAKE YOUR DAILY INTENTIONAL PRACTICE HAPPEN? FOR ME, IT'S A LOT OF SELF-RECRIMINATION, ANGER, REGRET, and generally being mean to myself. I'm usually angry that I've disappointed myself, and I often tack on the "yet again" refrain afterwards for good measure. I'm upset that I haven't achieved the goals I set for myself. I'm sad that I didn't do the thing that was good for me, that I actually wanted to do, and that would have made me happy. And I'm beyond disappointed in myself, because it becomes another reminder of all the times I've failed in the past. Unfortunately, I don't take the fact that I didn't do what I set out to do as an isolated incident; instead, it becomes part of a larger dialogue about me being a loser—and I start to believe those voices in my head again.

VOICES

You probably know those voices too, right? The ones full of self-doubt? The ones that said you could never do it in the first place? The ones that keep you from doing and getting the things you really want?

These are voices of fear, and trust me when I tell you, they are not real—and, most important, they are not right. Those voices are not the voices of people that care about you; they are not your friends and they will lie to you. They are not the voices on your square inch. So don't listen to them. Especially when they are incorrectly taking one instance of failure and making it into your everyday reality.

Those voices are lying to you because they are scared. They want things to stay the same. They don't want change. They want the easy thing and they are terrified of hard things. They will do or say anything to get you to believe them. There's no line they won't cross, and low blows are their regular playground.

My voices are all internal. I can be my own worst enemy far more than anyone else. I am proud that I am hard on myself and can drive myself harder than most—but I also know that I'm sometimes too hard on myself and often have unreasonable expectations about what I "should" accomplish.

Who are your voices? Where do they come from? Are they internal, like mine? Or do they come from people in your life, like your husband, sister, mom, or dad? Maybe it's a friend that wants the best for you, but the way it comes out is overly harsh, and rather than inspiring you to success, it scares you away from starting? Is there someone in your life that says they're supportive, but everything they actually do is completely unsupportive and the antithesis to what you're trying to accomplish?

Regardless of where your voices of fear and doubt come from, they are likely making it harder for you to do what you need to do in a consistent way to change your life; they may be directly or even subtly sabotaging your efforts to grow. Luckily, there's something that can help with those voices: compassion.

I have a strange and difficult relationship with that word, "compassion." For a very long time I thought it meant to have pity for someone, and associated it with weakness. Compassion was always a dirty word in my head because to me, there are few things worse than being pitied. I would get angry if someone said they were expressing compassion for me or anything close to it. I'm not sure how, when, or where it started, but a definite negative connotation was cemented in my head. For me, the word "compassion" essentially equaled being passive, and the only thing worse than being pitied was being thought of as passive or weak— or, even worse, actually *being* weak.

Showing or receiving compassion also meant being vulnerable—an even dirtier and far scarier word for me, if that was even possible. Vulnerability meant people could harm you—that you were an easy target. Being vulnerable and weak meant you were a victim, and that was something I most definitely did not want to be. From everything I learned as a kid, being a victim was not something anyone should aspire to be.

I'm not exactly sure where or how these thoughts were drilled into my head, but they certainly were, and for a long time there was no budging them.

THE TRUE MEANING OF COMPASSION

It was only when I started meditation and therapy that I truly learned the meaning of the word compassion and started to change my relationship to it.

According to Webster's dictionary, compassion is "the sympathetic consciousness of others' distress together with a desire to alleviate it." There are two parts of this definition that are worth further examination. Let's start by examining the first part: the idea of conscious awareness of the distress of others.

Being conscious of others' pain means being clued in, paying attention, and staying aware of what is happening to others. It requires active attention and being present. And being present, aware, and in the moment is the key to intentionality in our lives.

We often spend time going from moment to moment without ever stopping to be conscious of what is actually happening in the moment we're currently experiencing. One of the important elements to truly living is being present with each moment of every day. This is my goal for every day of my life: to be present and aware in each moment. I will be the first to tell you that I will never fully achieve that goal; being present takes a lot of focus and attention, and doing that in every moment of every day is pretty much impossible. Nevertheless, I practice it all the time, and even though I fail at it several times every day, I keep practicing. I use the goal of always being present to remind myself to do it as much as possible, because living each moment fully is the best gift I can give to myself.

Being present allows us to see those moments when others are in distress and in need of compassion. It's also a key to accomplishing your daily practice, because it compels you to think about how you're structuring life differently at times to make your practice happen. You will have to be present in those moments that you don't want to do it but know you can and should. And most importantly, being present it is what will help you in the first part of the definition of compassion: having an awareness about others' distress—and, I would add, your own distress. That is the start of exercising compassion, for yourself and others.

The second component of compassion is the desire to alleviate the distress you see. Why is this necessary or important? Because it is not enough to merely recognize other people's pain; compassion must also include the desire to do something about it. Note, however, that the definition of compassion doesn't say it is necessary to actually solve the problem or change the situation. Just the recognition of the pain and the desire to do something about it is all that is necessary.

So, what does that mean when it comes to compassion for yourself? It means recognizing that while you may always want to complete your daily intentional practice, there may be extenuating circumstances that will prevent you from doing so, and that learning to respond to those situations with compassion rather than with anger, disappointment, and regret is critical. Compassion is not something you should only offer to other people; you should also extend it to yourself. Making efforts to forgive yourself and be understanding with yourself is all part of the practice of self-compassion.

PRACTICE SELF-COMPASSION

Last year, when my daily intentional practice was reading ten pages a day, I got a bad case of food poisoning while traveling internationally during the holidays. I was out of it for an entire day, with nothing but sleep and bathroom time. I couldn't eat anything; the best I could do was drink some water and ginger ale.

At some point that afternoon, I picked up my book to get my pages in because I *had* to get my pages read for the day, but my eyes could barely focus well enough to see the words on the pages. I tried to push through anyway; after reading a few pages, however, I realized that I was not actually taking anything in, and although I was technically reading, I definitely was not having fun.

Reading had become something enjoyable for me again, so to recognize that although my eyes on were the pages, I wasn't *really* reading, and definitely not having fun, was a conscious moment for me. I may have been following the letter of the law of my daily practice, but I clearly wasn't following the spirit or, more important, the *intention*, of my daily practice. The point of my daily intentional practice is to add something positive to my life, not to torture myself for the sake of saying I've done something.

Realizing this, I put the book down and tried to get some rest. But I will admit that as I drifted off to sleep, I still felt guilty about not finishing my reading for the day.

That is when I decided to practice some self-compassion.

Compassion is something I have been trying to work through for a long time. While by this point I was at a place where I could "let myself off the hook" for something legitimate like being sick, I still carried a lot of judgment and guilt when I didn't do the things I was "supposed" to do. I knew learning to be patient and compassionate with myself was important—not just for me but for the people I love. I had grown to understand that being so hard on myself wasn't just about the way I treated myself, it was also about the way I treated others. There is a direct correlation between the amount of flexibility and compassion you show yourself and the amount you're willing to give to others.

I never believed that the tough standard I held for myself was the same one I unconsciously held others to, until my therapist challenged me on it. When I took the time to stop and really examine it, the evidence was right there, staring me in the face.

PRACTICE COMPASSION FOR OTHERS

I hate being late to anything. Meetings, movies with friends, dinner—if I arrive late to anything that I'm supposed to be at by a certain time, I get genuinely upset with myself. To me, being late is rude; it's disrespectful of others' time and efforts.

While there may be some truth to this idea, it is not always that simple. Sometimes you leave early and traffic is far worse that you expected. Sometimes you're ready on time but a call comes in at the last minute that you have to take, or something else happens that you just have to deal with. And sometimes people are prone to running late because they're poor planners and don't give themselves enough time to get somewhere.

Truth be told, the reason doesn't matter, because I often get upset with others in the same way I get with myself when it comes to being late. And while I'm not someone who yells or screams at people, it is clear to anyone who's looking that I'm not pleased with them if they've arrived late to meet me. I am definitely not as outwardly hard on other people as I am with myself internally, but I could definitely employ more compassion for others in those situations.

The small ways that I need to work on being compassionate with myself and others, like with being late, translate to the big things as well—the things that require tremendous amounts of forgiveness, empathy, and/or compassion. And if I've learned anything through my daily intentional practice over the years, it's that if you can't get the small things right, the big things will seem impossible. So build on the small things you need to work on with regard to compassion and you'll find yourself in a much better and happier place. Just like we build off of small wins as we incorporate daily practice in our life, we can build off of our small efforts to demonstrate compassion and flexibility. In the long run, they will go a long way toward making it a habit, which will make it easier to demonstrate these qualities in all areas of our lives.

SELF-COMPASSION IS NOT A FREE PASS

I've also learned that compassion and vulnerability are so far from fear, they are actually the opposite: they are acts of bravery. To be able to put yourself out there and express the most vulnerable things you're feeling and thinking takes a lot of courage. Not everyone has that ability, and it is something I am constantly working on—but again, it is so worth it if you're able to do it.

I do want to caution that showing yourself compassion as you go through your daily practice doesn't mean you get a pass to not work hard. Yes, you should give yourself room to make a mistake or not do everything you wanted to do, but there is a big difference between "I'm not feeling it today, so I'm just not going to do it" and "I was in a car accident and really can't walk my mile today." It is important to distinguish between these two situations, and it's vital to be honest and clear with yourself about which one you're actually experiencing in the moment.

You took on this daily practice for a reason; you want to succeed because you know the benefits you will get will be worth it and far outweigh whatever momentary discomfort you might be going through. So be clear-eyed, honest, and present when you are presented with those extremely rare moments when it seems like you can't get your practice in. Don't use self-compassion as an excuse to give yourself the easy way out when you just don't feel like pushing yourself. When you look back later and realize that you could have done it, you'll regret taking the path of least resistance. And we know that wasting that time on regret is not worth it.

NO REGRETS

In those tough moments, one thing I like to do is close my eyes and ask myself that exact question: *Will I regret this decision tomorrow?* In those moments when you want to give up, when it seems like you can't do what you need to, ask yourself if you will regret quitting tomorrow, or even in a few hours. As the year goes on and your daily practice gets easier and easier to complete, the answer to that question will become clearer with very little internal debate. Spell out the barriers that you believe are keeping you from your daily practice in this moment and then work on breaking through those barriers.

You think you don't have enough time? If you have time to debate it, you have time to do it. Get it done. Is it just that you're not feeling it that day? Go back and look at your past accomplishments. However you're tracking your day-to-day success, go back and look at your check marks, your daily scores, your smiley faces or stickers. Whatever you've decided to use to mark your accomplishment each day, go back and look at that and remember how you pushed through all those times before. Remind yourself there were days in there when you thought you weren't going to make it, but you did. Tell yourself that right now and get your practice in.

Another tactic I like to use is to set up a special reward for those moments when you really don't want to do it and it seems even harder to push through. What is that special reward that you can promise yourself in that moment that will get you over the hump? This isn't part of your regular reward system. This is a rare, once-in-a-while, really special reward for pushing through today, this moment. So make it count.

When you have a genuine desire to complete your daily practice but circumstances prevent you from doing it, let it go and gear yourself up to come back and fight another day.

Genuine desire, awareness, presence, and true effort are what I ask of myself. I encourage you to ask and give the same of yourself. Once you're able to look yourself in the eyes and truly say you have a genuine desire, are conscious of what you're doing in the moment, and have made a real effort using any and all of the suggestions above, give yourself room to let it go for the day and start focusing on what you're going to do differently tomorrow to be successful. Remember, each new day we're alive is gift and another opportunity to grow and succeed at our daily intentional practice.

14.

Always Be Starting

IF YOU'VE SEEN THE MOVIE *Glengarry Glen Ross*, YOU PROBABLY KNOW THE PHRASE, "ABC: ALWAYS BE CLOSING." IT'S A MANTRA THAT ALEC BALDWIN'S SALESMAN CHARACTER brings to life in a glorious, expletive-filled, and oh-so-memorable monologue. In the movie's context, "Always Be Closing" means you should always be ready to close a new sale at any moment, no matter what you're doing.

For our purposes, our focus is not on closing a sale but on something much more important: beginnings. So I've switched it up to ABS: Always Be Starting.

I try to apply this lesson in two different ways. First, there's no need to wait until the start of a new year, or a new week, or even tomorrow to start your daily intentional practice. You can start right now. This moment. Yes, this second. Why not put this book down and go ahead and do your ten pushups or take your walk around the block or do whatever it is that you've been putting off? Turn your brain off, along with any excuses you can think of, and use this opportunity to *do*, not think. Embrace the power of not thinking and not torturing yourself anymore by not procrastinating further. Just doing is amazing. Don't think, just get to doing it. I'll wait.

Okay, so you're back having completed today's practice, right? Nice job! Always Be Starting means that you don't have to wait until January 1 (or some other magical day) to start your journey. Your journey can start the second you become aware of what you need to do and have the necessary resources to do it. If your practice is to ride a bike each day and you don't have a bike yet, you may want to get one first, but the moment you have that bike, get started.

Most of us humans like to put things off and procrastinate because it's easier and we're a little lazy—or we're scared, or we don't think we can do it. But just like sky diving (full disclosure: I haven't done it), you have to take a deep breath and just jump out of the plane. If you're always ready to start, you'll always be in control of when and how to get going, versus letting circumstances control you.

FINE-TUNE

Another reason not to wait for a date in the future is that getting started as soon as possible gives you an opportunity to try things out and make adjustments as necessary. As I've already mentioned, I always know the first few weeks of January are going to be pretty tough because I'm still figuring out how to incorporate this new habit into my life. Whether it's determining what time of the day (morning versus night) or how or where I'm going to incorporate my daily practice, there's usually some amount of adjustment that needs to happen—so if I can, I try to start practicing in December, so I can experiment and work out those kinks without being "on the clock," so to speak.

I started reading in December of 2015 so I could ease myself back into the habit of reading before I officially started in January of 2016. I did some writing in December of 2016 before starting my daily writing practice in 2017. Both times, getting the jump on the new practice made a difference in my confidence level when the year officially started. I was able to try out different approaches until I found one that worked for me, and that made me confident going in that I had the right rhythm and could make my daily intentional practice a part of my life.

The other reason to always be ready to start is that each new day you're alive is a gift that you've been given. When you wake up and are able to draw a breath, however you draw that breath, you have a new opportunity to meet your challenge. If you're in the mindset of being ready to start each moment of each day, then you've already succeeded—you're already ahead. I am constantly looking to make sure I've set myself up for success and that I'm always ready to start each day of life I'm given each year.

And that Always Be Starting attitude doesn't just apply to January 1. I try to take that into every single day of the year when it comes to my daily intentional practice by using all the tools and suggestions I've given you in this book.

So, how do you make sure that you're always ready to start? You guessed it: by going back to the key for everything. Always Be Starting requires being mindful of all that you're doing and why you're doing it. It requires recognizing that consciousness and awareness is the starting point of anything that you want to be successful at—especially your daily intentional practice. That same mindfulness that you bring to your overall practice applies to every area of your life. It starts by truly understanding the habit loop and how you developed the ones you currently have.

UNDERSTANDING YOUR WHY

Adjusting your routine only happens when you're aware of what that routine actually is—and because most habits have become automatic, we often don't take the time to examine them. Once you've stopped to examine not only *what* you do but *why* you're doing it, you can start to make change happen.

Understanding your why for everything you do comes from being mindful and doing the critical examination and analysis I talked about earlier. Once you have a grasp on your reasons, you can change your existing habits and hopefully add new ones that will make you a happier and more fulfilled person. By replacing the routine in your existing habits, or creating new routines and rewards, you too can create a daily intentional practice (or several) that enhances your life.

After you've become mindful of habits you currently have and how you want to change them, start with small wins so you can taste a bit of success and build on it. Those wins can be in the form of a shorter time goal, like a week or a month, or in your accomplishing part of the overall goal that you're trying to achieve—walking half a mile versus a full mile, for example.

SURRENDER TO TRIAL AND ERROR

Give yourself room to "fail" and improve. I put quotation marks around "fail" because there's no failing in practice; there is only improving and fine-tuning. You can have a good day of practice or a bad day, but simply going out there and doing it means you're already winning, because you're using the power of practice to change.

Find the ways that work best for you by testing several elements, like different times of day and alternative structures in your life, so you'll know what to do differently in order to ensure your daily intentional practice will happen. Give yourself the flexibility to figure out your road to success. Tell yourself it's a test, an experiment, and give yourself room to figure things out as you go. It's not about perfection as much as it's about refining your formula for success a little bit more each and every day.

Tell yourself it will likely be hard as you figure out the formula. And be sure to tell yourself it's going to get easier as well, especially as you keep it up. Along the way, if you hone your powers of perception and awareness, you'll build your practice piece by piece, getting better and stronger along the way. Hopefully you'll be enjoying yourself and having fun as well; keep in mind, your daily intentional practice should be enjoyable and not a burden. So stop and check in with yourself throughout and ask if you're still having fun. Are you enjoying yourself? Is your practice enhancing your life? If not, look for ways to change that and get the fun back.

PREP FOR SUCCESS

Set yourself up for success throughout by doing what you need to do to make your practice happen. Go to bed an hour earlier. Wake up ten minutes earlier. Take your book with you to dinner. Pack your running shoes in your bag the night before. Set yourself up for success because you know that's what you truly want.

One of the biggest challenges to completing a daily

intentional practice is that most of us don't have enough time. But honestly, you know you have more time than you think. There is enough time. Go back to the Holstee manifesto and take its advice. Stop watching mindless TV. Stop losing fifteen minutes mindlessly scrolling through Facebook or Instagram or Snapchat. That's your time so, don't steal it from yourself with activities that you're not truly present to and engaged with. Be conscious of the moment you're in and use that time to focus on the things you really want to do; give that time back to yourself in the form of your daily intentional practice.

Sometimes you just need to turn your brain off. Life is hard. Maybe you've had a really tough day at work or with the kids. Maybe you've had a fight with your significant other. Maybe, damn it, you *need* that glass of wine or *The Real Housewives* or *The Bachelor* or, my personal favorite, *Married At First Sight*. But what if you gave yourself fifteen minutes first? Just fifteen minutes to complete your practice and get closer to where and what you want to be? That's just a quarter of an hour. What if every day you took that amount of time to do the thing you really wanted to do? How could that change your life?

Again, on those days when it just seems like you can't do it anymore, go back and look at why you started this in the first place. Read through your reasons and remember the desire that kicked this off. Repeat your mantras to evoke the feeling you had when you first created them. Think about your short-term and long-term rewards. Go back and pull out the list of rewards you wrote down earlier. Do you still want them? They are only a few moments away. Get going and you will be there.

EMBRACE RESILIENCE

When you've given it your best effort on the toughest of days and you just can't make your practice happen, remember your compassion. Be kind to yourself and nurture yourself after you've done everything you can to fulfill your goal. And in addition to your compassion, embrace resilience.

According to Webster's dictionary, one of the definitions of resilience is "an ability to recover from or adjust easily to misfortune or change." One of the most underdeveloped skills most of us possess is our ability to bounce back from disappointment. There's an ongoing debate around resilience and whether it's a skill that can be improved over time or an innate trait that one has or doesn't have—but for my part, I believe the capacity to recover from setbacks is a muscle that can be improved, just like a physical muscle in your body. If you work your legs with squats and box jumps and deadlifts, your legs will get stronger. If you work at bouncing back when difficulties arise, you will get stronger and over time, better at it.

While no one *wants* bad things to happen to them, those that embrace those circumstances and develop their ability to not only deal with them but come back stronger and smarter are the ones who are really living. You can probably think of people who have gone through tragic circumstances—perhaps the death of a child or a battle with cancer—and carry an air of strength and power that is almost visible. That is what comes from being resilient and using the challenges in life to make you better.

Your ability to be resilient will not only come in handy during your daily intentional practice, it will be tested and hopefully strengthened throughout it. This is a great way to strengthen your response to setbacks. When you can't complete your daily practice, and you use that moment to come back the next day and tackle it again, this is your resilience muscle getting stronger— and it's you demonstrating your ability to Always Be Starting. When you don't meet all the goals you've set for yourself but you don't quit, that's your resilience muscle getting stronger. When instead of using small failures as an opportunity to beat yourself up or say negative things to yourself, or quit for good, you use them as an opportunity to start again, that's resilience.

It goes both ways: your daily intentional practice can increase your resilience even as you use your resilience to continue and improve your daily practice. And remember, it all begins with Always Be Starting.

15.
Parting Words

THIS HAS BEEN MY JOURNEY; IT'S WHAT I'VE LEARNED OVER THE COURSE OF THE LAST SEVEN YEARS. I WANTED TO SHARE THIS WITH YOU BECAUSE I KNOW HOW MUCH OF A difference my daily practice has made in my life and I wanted to help give that to others. I hope you will embark on your own journey, learn your own lessons, and create your own success. Remember to focus on doing it your way and finding those tools and tactics that are right for you. Each year I start a new daily intentional practice, I learn something new about myself and discover different ways to not only enhance my ability to do my daily practice but my enjoyment of it as well.

WHAT COMES NEXT

When I started all of this I wasn't thinking beyond what I was doing in the moment, and I certainly didn't think

I would be able to keep it going this long. But I have, because every year there's something new that excites and energizes me all over again. I wouldn't have been able to keep this up for the past seven years if that wasn't the case.

When I share my daily practice with others, the two questions I get most often are: 1) Do you still do the practices you've done in past years? and 2) What comes next/how long are you going to do this?

The answer to the first question is mostly yes. I have incorporated many of my daily practices from previous years into my day-to-day life. I give myself the freedom to stop anything once I begin a new daily intentional practice on January 1 of the following year, but I also ask myself if I want to make the previous daily practice a part of my life going forward. Specifically, I ask, *Does the practice serve me?*

Even if the answer is yes and I keep practicing, I don't put pressure on myself to continue doing so for the rest of my life. As long as the practice continues to serve me, enhance my life, and make me happy, I will continue it. At the same time, I am not committed to doing something that didn't naturally become a habit over 365 days of practicing. I don't, for example, currently eat one serving of vegetables every day. In fact, I sometimes specifically make a point of avoiding veggies on Fridays, because it's a Friday and I just don't want to eat them. And no, I don't stretch every day. I certainly do eat more vegetables than I did before, however, and I definitely stretch more than I did before my daily stretch practice, too. And while I don't actively write down one thing I'm grateful for each day anymore, I do often try to reframe whatever is happening from a place of gratitude.

DAILY TEN

Most of the practices I have been adding to my life over the past few years are things that make me happy—and why wouldn't I want to do more of that? Last year I sat down and asked myself what I needed or wanted to do each day to make me feel fulfilled and content. As a friend I once knew would often say, "What makes your heart feel full?"

I call the list I put together my "Daily Ten," and it includes simple activities throughout the day that give me true happiness—things that put a real smile on my face and fill me with a sense of completeness. A few of these activities include working out, meditating, and writing—all three of which are things I've brought into my life through my daily intentional practice. These practices have transformed my life and my overall happiness in profound ways. This doesn't mean that I *must* do those things every day, but I try to use the list to ground myself and as a reminder of what I truly want and what is important to me.

BE BRAVE

One of the most important aspects of starting a daily practice that I haven't discussed yet is bravery. Being brave is an extremely important part of this process and can't be overlooked. Just like you need to acknowledge any fear you have, you also need to tap into that courageous part of you that has the ability to show strength in the face of fear or difficulty. Bravery as you even dare to undertake a daily intentional practice. Bravery on those days when things are difficult and it feels like you're not going to get your practice done. Bravery in not shrinking from who you are and who you can be. Bravery in not giving in to your fear of past failures. Bravery in leaning into the strength you know you have. And bravery in telling others about your daily intentional practice and inviting them to help you with their support. Your courageousness throughout your practice will help you get to where you want to be.

YOU ARE ENOUGH

As someone who has struggled through self-esteem issues at different points in my life, one of the toughest lessons I've had to learn is the phrase "I Am Enough." I don't know when I originally heard this phrase, but I know that I've definitely repeated it at times when I didn't believe it. Whether it was when I had trouble believing that my partner really loved me or not thinking I was good enough at work, I definitely went through many years when I was faking it. Some will tell you to fake it until you make it; that may work for some people, but for me it was important to try and understand why I felt like I wasn't enough and to counter that feeling.

Once again, it starts with awareness and being present. Asking myself tough questions about why I thought I wasn't enough required me to really examine what was going on and separate the fear from the truth. The more I dug into it, the more I realized that I truly was enough. I was smart enough, pretty enough, and thin enough; I was worthy of love as I was.

There are moments when I start to doubt the truth in those words. Those are the times I go back to asking questions and getting intentional about why I think I'm not enough. And when I answer the question with the *facts* of who I am and what I've accomplished, I know the truth is that I am enough. I'm a realist and I always have been; I don't blow smoke up my ass or anyone else's. So now when I say I am enough, I know it's not something I'm faking or telling myself just to feel better. I have the evidence to prove it. It is the truth.

So if I really am enough, why embark on a mission to get "better" each year? Doesn't being enough mean I'm good as is?

This takes us back to the central purpose of adopting a daily intentional practice. It begins with a starting point of recognizing that you're not doing this for someone else or because you think you're lacking. You're doing this because you've identified something that you want to bring into your life. That is why the focus is on *adding* a new practice or habit, versus trying to restrict or punish yourself. Each year, my daily intentional practice focuses on finding activities that will enhance my life in a positive way. I'm looking for something that will add to my "I Am Enough" in a meaningful way. It doesn't have to be something that will change my life from day to night, but it will be something that overall makes me a happier person. And note that I said *happier*, not necessarily *happy*. If you start a daily intentional practice from an unhappy place and try to use your practice as a way to make yourself happy, you may not find success.

TRUST THE PROCESS

It wasn't until recently that I learned the key to my daily intentional practice is the process itself, not the end goal. You may have started this book to figure out how to keep your New Year's resolutions and transform your life, but here's the twist: in order to meet that goal, you can't focus on the goal itself. Rather, you must focus on the process of getting there. As they say, it's the journey, not the destination. That saying may be trite and clichéd, but it's also true.

More accurately, the most important piece of this

whole endeavor are the *steps along the journey*. The steps, not the goal, are what change you.

Every day that you get up and practice intentionally you're changing yourself—and while you are getting closer to where you want to be, you'll never be *there*. And that's because *there* isn't a destination one can ever really achieve. It's not "practice makes perfect," because there's no such thing as perfect. It is "practice makes better." It is "practice makes possible." Because all the things you want will be possible when you practice with intention each day of your life.

So how do we balance the desire to change, the desire to attain certain goals, with a focus on the journey, the process? By working on our ability not to get attached to the end and the outcome, and by concentrating on just one step at a time, recognizing how each step gets us closer to where we want to be. Just like a baby that moves from crawling to holding on to items to eventually standing and walking, each step in the process is crucial and should be celebrated.

When a caterpillar becomes a butterfly, each part of its transition is crucial; it's those small moments of change that result in the massive transformation. The caterpillar isn't focused on becoming a butterfly, it's simply going through its natural growth process, step by step. Be like the caterpillar; don't let yourself get overly attached to the end goal. Instead, focus on making each day what you want it to be.

When you are intentional with your time and efforts and mindful about working toward what you want and need in life, you will get there. If you're only focused on the goal itself, however, you may miss out on all the valuable experiences along the way and not even get to where you want to go. Remember, it's the intentional journey, not the ultimate destination.

As I said, my Daily Ten is a list of some of the things I need and want to engage in each day in order to be happy. It's no accident that it includes some of the daily intentional practices I've done over the past few years, including daily meditation, reading each day, and, now, writing. My daily intentional practice has helped me determine what makes me feel happy and fulfilled in my life, and finding ways to incorporate those things into my day-to-day world has changed not only my outlook and disposition, but who I am.

What's your Daily Ten? Take a moment to sit down and think about what makes you happy and fills your heart. I began this process as a way to get "better," but ultimately it did so much more for me; it led me to transform my life and become a happier and more fulfilled person. To me, that's an even better result. Isn't that always one of the goals we strive for, to be happier in our lives with who we are and what we do?

By the way, I wrote this book using my daily intentional writing practice—one day at a time, bit by bit—and now I've completed another life goal. See?

Anything is possible. Isn't it time you got started with your daily practice?

Good luck, and I know you can do it!

Acknowledgements

THIS BOOK HAS BEEN A DREAM OF MINE FOR SOME TIME AND I'M GRATEFUL AND AMAZED THAT IT'S FINALLY COME TO FRUITION. AS WITH MOST THINGS IN LIFE, I DIDN'T do it alone. In addition to all the friends and loved ones who encouraged me along the way I want to say a special thank you to a few people who helped bring *Power of Practice* to life:

Brooke Warner and Warner Coaching. In addition to the great editing work she and her team provided, Brooke was the first person to read a draft and tell me I actually had something worth sharing. Thank you Brooke for the great work and encouragement.

Kim Dow and DowHouse Graphic Design. Thank you for the fantastic cover, amazing visuals and your general brilliance. Thank you for making this happen.

Angela Sebastiana. I don't have the words to properly

thank you for all the brunches, coffees, sessions in the car and long, random text exchanges that kept me going over the past year. Your love, advice, guidance and laughter have been heaven sent and I'm thankful for your existence on this planet every day. Let's make BoCoDoCo happen already!

Kamy Wicoff. Thank you for gently encouraging me to pursue this crazy idea over a random dinner in 2016. Who knew that your off-hand comment would turn into this? I also want to thank you for introducing me to Brooke years ago during the *Wishful Thinking* book tour.

A special thank you to all the friends who have been so supportive, listening to my stories and living these stories with me: Lisa, Eunice, Sarah, Isobel, Ron, MaryRose, Ellis & Harper, Katina, Erin, Jay, Emily, Stephanie, Laura, Jodi. And lastly, Counselor Troi — I couldn't, and wouldn't, have written this without you. Thank you and I love you all.

If you want to learn more about my 2018 Kindness Daily Intentional Practice, or starting one of your own, check out my website at saydeahhoward.com.

Thanks for reading and good luck on your journey!

22208197R00119

Made in the USA
San Bernardino, CA
09 January 2019